[bat.country] version 2.0

>>

//_bat.country Ver.1.2 - created 24-8-2014
//+bat.country Ver.0.1 - created 24-8-2014

- this version features previous editions & for functionality purposes
  omits images and some registry files included in earlier versions:

Contents
_welcome
list.x
story_file

bat_country
    adelle_index
        ad_MSG

        list-breach
            index_001
            trans_01
        list-truth
            index
            key
            list
        adelle_index
        adelle_mod##
        file_list

    dicentra_
        _SCN.112.332
            ReSCN_dicentra
            SCN.dicentra
            scn_9007
            SCN_dicentra
            scn_s
            scn_xx
            SCNXY
            SCNXY773
            SCNXY774
            SCNXY_
        codex
        dicentra_warning
        dicentra_yin

    file.precis
        file_precis

    heine-index
        .delilah_file
        heine_system
        key_file
        key_index

    memory-file
        all_meaning
            _terminal
                portal.list
                    _terminal
                _boot
                data
                file
                index
                monitor
                terminalhope
            allmeaning_ruins
            blu33f
            heartbleed-cert
            heartbleed-drm
            indexfix

```
        mod##0987
        mod##0988
        ruins_mod
        senate8082
        U5terminus
dream+system
        _file_001
        _file_7
        _file_8
        _file_191
        _file_193
        _file_1398
        _file_1946
        _file_3332_991818
        _file_8082
        _file_goldenhawk
        _file_recover
        chain_file_7112
        choifall
        direction0
        dreamfile#3
        list.index
        lydiasenate
        playlist
        precis.photo
        project_hiero773
        project_hiero774
        truthTTE
        tvtv
        Untitled332
exit-file
        terminal.exit
mod-file
        _mod_2_x
        _mod_recover
        _re_mod_2
        b_c_monitor
        codexZ
        dicentra.warning
        j=ig_##
        j=ig_recover
        mod##0987
        mod##0988
        ruins
        system
        xx_yin
        xy_yin
system-file
        _delivery
                2_117
                11.0-11thsighting
                11.1
                11.2
                11.3
                11.4
                11.5
                11.6
                11.7
                11thsighting.chart
                plnetfile
        [system]church
```

```
                    +++.system
                    church[system]
                    console.monitor
                    file.PSYC
                    file

       temp.file
             13##file
             all_files
             b_c.cc.tv_

       b_c_file
       codec
       data
       Untitled565
       untitledZ
```

direction 0

```
       air_quest
             0_batch_index
             web_direct

       re_story
             2014-08-24 10.39.31oilspill_
             8876list
             audioTRNS
             audioTRNS2
             sleeping giant
             The Basis'
       codextrans
       codexZ
       dicentra.yin2
       indexfix
       poke_file
       R_SCN.dicentra
       R_SCN1.dicentra
       share
       soyValla
       soyVallaII
       taxaref
       taxascn
       time_stop
       time_trance
       tvskywardannouncement
       two+
       Untitled565
```

```
[bat.country] version 1.2
welcome to bat.country_
```

your new life starts here!

"as the city of Lydia falls, the king promises freedom to his people - the way forward is the future!"

__join now to be a part of the first leap!___

'turmoil has governed our country, and fear, our people - for too long! join us on a path to the future, a journey to our salvation!'

'Lydia is no longer our home... to move forwards is our destiny!'

'do not fear my people! the 60 year leap takes our civilisation into the future, and beyond! i, your king will keep you safe - as we travel to our new life!'

_the 60 year leap! a way into the future!__

>>>bat.country_##/:

>
>

```
>>//:list.x/:file.
```

```
c:/all hope was lost
fear and loathing was on tv
i had tuned in... just in time
i thought; where was i going, what had i done...

i sat outside, watching the screen through the sliding glass door.

i can take another photo of myself - an image... look what we've become.
why am i awake? it is 5:40am. i saw a weather balloon, it floated across
the sky. not like the ufo which took off with haste, disappearing into the
night sky, drifting amongst the stars - returning near to me, until i was
home. i was out of the city, a long way... and i was high; sleep deprived,
driving through the night, having not seen a soul in over an hour.


i am out of cigarettes - and i have seen time slow to a stop before me.


today i painted on the walls of the city. black squares and green zigzags,
green squares and black static.
i was moving into a new apartment; Northside - and with a balcony... the
apartment fell through, and i was stuck in a room stinking of bongs.

they call me King. [N]<
'meta punk dropped by, didn't leave a msg.'

+++ "i'm always late... sometimes blue. that is so fried. eh, moving
along..."

++who am i playing?
+who is up?

King isn't a queen. [o]<

the clouds are moving across the sky. the earth spins.

[Z]<

people are dancing. tom yum soup; r.m#o, CHOKO++

levels; bases. freedom_ illegal. playlist. list of ep's.

>[+]
freedom;
full. love, fear- fear/ love, fear.
_')/

>[O]

(
++
++++++
^^no.
god damn, no.
madness, rivalry. oblique.

[Z]<


c:/batcountry
```

madness; another place. FLWR->-* needs water. r.m3o moves regardless, and
it's all things everywhere.
[Z]<
choko+++++
++++++
&it's all and a heaven, pays to; a castle, bells ringing. +++++++
+++
[W]<
#hashtag; madness, rivalry; sensations, fields, mountains, valleys, water.
oblique. another place ~ sex and ++++++
[V]<
#my dice rolls 16, volcano stones; glasses & fullsick, nausea, too many
weapons, zig-zags; tv remote.
color-palette, colour palette,
++++++++++++++++
f:/labyrinth; oblique. Seizures, epilepsy, zig-zags, tv, remote, nausea,
full, sick, glass, stone, volcano, 16, rolls... my; dice - colour, ... ++
remote; personal, channels, frequencies; nausea... who rolls?
labyrinth.
[X]<

#hashtag; oblique; RoM3. eats a bread roll, things move, in space, tv, 0-
16, outpsyjah, labyrinth, seizures, epilepsy, ziz-zags, full, sick, glass,
stone, volcano, 16, outside/-r and the outside.

tv - remote, t.v. brains, bRaInZ. r*m3o; trance, brains, trance, zig-zags,
trance, tv, trance.
labyrinth, in the belly of a whale/shark
c:/shark
trance. epilepsy, seizures, labyrinth, brains, in the belly, zig-zags, and
the inside,
#hashtag #chokotvrebelbroadcast #outpsyjah #outpsyjah')/ #choko #tv #art
#trance #techno #organtrail #r.m3. #CHOKO #[Z]< #gum #surrealism #CHOKO++++
#boddah #cool #timepasses #untitled #rest #aliens invade!!! #frog/bug #atom
furnace #free fall #trance #e-sides #0-16 #iosaf #vlpyn #KP #KLKL #kramer
lives! kramer loves! #kramer's place #merv-griffen show #bungalow/Smash
shit #is Static _playlist #0-6 #7 #8 #9-16

c:/horizons

>tetris.flower
>kaleidoscopes
>meta, more, psy, see;
>1, 2

[Z]<

c:/dry scalp
ultimate beauty, watch forever, 1; free licence, two-step-procedure to fix-
your-life, #hashtag.

c:/pizza

+++
c:/rebellion

[Z]<
[ ]<

pizza, pepsi, pepsi max, on the road, the tibetan book of living and dying,
secret places, 32, 4, magic, boddah's cool, toe-sculptures, pizza,

labyrinth, trance, house of leaves; black and white edition, published
2000; full colour edition, no publish date; water, smellovision, pizza,
nameless protagonist.

King is amused.

inability to speak, like a dog; to respond. [Z]<

trance.

doof music, spirals, wormholes, vortex, spirals, kaleidoscopes, rebellion,
purple-sky, zombie movies, the Whalestoe, Daybreak, the agents, sayain,
experiments, bridges, drawing pictures, painting walls, books, videogames,
star wars, climatic disappointment, star wars, and the trek.

trance.

r.m#o, CHOKO++++++++++++++
++++++++++++++
[Z]<

parallel universes open in all directions and possibly from a single
source. time is multi-fold and dimensions,
waves, trance, electricity and barbed wire.

++

c:/we can't stop here
[Z]<

King is a regular, he knows the Meta_Punk through art, and conversation,
bias.
nihil;division - nicotine. and the instrument/station nexus.
++++++
++++
++static++++++
++++++++++

[X]<
aliens;
++++++memory erasure, we have been avoiding for years.
+++aliens, paranoia, tv, the remote, pieces, batteries, trance,
technological advancement and the advent of techno. the sewer, spaceships
and tunnels while maggotbrain and the rain falls; spiders make webs in the
architraves,
aliens.

c:/t.v cult
>hidden; King takes a beer, something on t.v, no batteries, videogames,
paranoia, aggression, occult, and the
overwhelming desire to experi+++++++++ have sensation+++
+++
+++
+++++++++++t.v+++++++++++++++++++++++++++++++static++++++++++++

_____

c:/t.v; [$]<
endless channels, King's gaze, no batteries, +++++, choko++++++, paranoia,
victor. takeaway containers. King demands something of me, like he has [Z]<

[9]

c:/love and rest; the Meta-Punk knows me, but cannot know, not really. He
can see and might believe. King has desire, fear and the other deliquencies
that most and rebel individuals refer to; [Z]<

c:/cassete and the source of all entertainment; set to flames. my
signature. [Z]<

c:/endless rants; irridescent and tragic, the end, blue.
c:/rebellion; all control, TMNT comics, secret documents.

King beckons me elsewhere. I do not follow. rebellion; secret, [Z]<

terminals; late night tapping, making tea, static. shopping, wash and
repeat, sport.
+++++++valency - balance, visualizers, enough to keep me entertained; to
pass through time - sleeping on the floor, bad backs. self-expression. too
many items and asian girlfriends. I appreciate Godot's path to a tree, and
Lord of the Flies
is a sick reference. +++++++++++++++++++++++++++

c:/the Hubble Telescope
terminals+++++++++ <messages

each time you convince a horny guy to sign up at a free webcam site we pay
you $15

here is a training manual so you can see how easy it is

most people make over $200 a day doing it. and we have paid out over
$90,000 this past year alone

want to actually make money online? do it with xxxxxxxxdollar.com

terminals;
>delete
>[Z]

c:/Feer
feelings of entrapment, foreclosure, misshapen foresight - about the depth
of polarity and whether it is necessary to achieve.
terminals; - sustained happiness, instable, fluctuations. _illegal
momentary justification or a sense of glee and an unknowing and a greater
knowing.
_____
  _____
  _____
  _____
  _____
  _____
  _____-__

++++++++++

our veins, when I was me.conversation with satan over the shower and
drunken bids. +++
art.directory_
>[Z]

_my.xxxxxxxxxxx
>unwilling to convene with King, I seek refuge only in the queen. [?].
+++++++++++++++++++ shades of grey, magic; the undead in hordes and their
base. gore and chans... +++++++++++ vidya//

c:/time/death/abhorrence
[V]<
pinning ideas to walls, allowing time to spin. Feer said "leave me alone",
or something along the lines of leave and let me rule. prawns in my rice,
and trance. smoking _cones/ great vortex and consumption for the greater
populous, masses, bells; "leave me alone", and I once was a child - burning
fuel, burning across the desert, anarchy; burning. *_cones leads to ample
mind space and max headroom*
>the unusual and phenomena; chokers and chicks in black with colourful
hair; platforms too thick to walk in... catching Z's _cones avoiding King,
for he is Feer++++++

c:/don't talk to strangers
>++
>how near is time? 5:35am - 7 days; yo-yo's and air rifles. Slug
guns,broken machines... 70's style tape recorders and game console. in some
sense all things are plugged in... King is himself and i am the scene...
t.v is addictive and you're all junkies. [Z]<

>>_/:no.controller//:<<

c:/CHOKO+++
[Z]<

'...r.m3.'

you engage the King.
Fight? Goods? Special? Do You Run?
King looks you in the eye!

[Z]<
+
+++++++
+
++___
[X]<
++
+
+++
+_
+
[K]<
+
++__+++

'RoM3o...'
'..ZZZZZZZZZZ...'

'we probably need to look out for boddah...'

[11]

'are we searching for skulls?'
'green ones?'

'we've died so many times!'

'...ZZZZZZ......'
+++

c:/freedom/rebellion/Z/+++/boddah/
'it's hard work putting half the globe in a trance.'
'tiresome.'
'totally!'

c:/freedom/love
[Z]<

c:/->-*

You found a present!
You found a present!
I am the hero in this game, it doesn't really make sense, but most people
claim to have painted the elephant on the water-tank, I went to the city.

c:/emptyspace
c:/King/bling/experiment
'It was her!'

c:/++97/july/16th:5:18am
'I was awake. It was my birthday. I was possibly in hospital, with a broken
leg.'

The King appeared!
He has been drinking... with the Meta Punk, Shadow King and dreamghost..!
what do you want to do?
King is drunk..!
'I know right..?'
>trance.
King is hungry.. He invites you to his banquet!

'we can go if you like..'

>trance.

c:/againstnature/trance/king'sbanquet/

King invites you to sit down. we feast on delicious food. music is playing.
everyone is merry...
'welcome to my palace! I hope you have enjoyed the food!'

Feer grabs a chicken leg, and starts eating.

the Meta Punk laughs, the dreamghost dance...

c:/againstnaure/trance/7thdimension
'I know right..!'
>trance.

++++++

[Z]<

'...ZZZZZZZZZZZZZZ..'
'r.m30000.....!'
'outpsyjah15,9-16,outpsyjah,outpsyjah')/'
'why didn't we go to the 5th dimension?'
'I don't know.'
'did you see that cult? they were painting themselves blue... and zombies!'

The King appears!
'Did you enjoy my banquet?'
'..ZZZZZZZZ......'
r.m3o thanks the King.

[Z]<

c:/pizza/pepperoni/

c:/empty space

...++++++++
++++++++++++
++_++_+++_+

..bRaInZ..!
'ah!'
c:/home/2070
FLWR->-@ is mad at us for trekking mud & dirt into the apartment... 'We're sorry.'
'TV Skyward will be here soon... +++++++
+++++++++_____<<<
>>>>>>>>>>>>>>>>>
<<<<<<<<<<<<<<<<
**r.Me0..'
[Z]<<<<<<<<<<
'..my tom yum has gotten cold.. I have beef noodle so+++++++++
+++++++++++++++++++
ZZZZZZZZZZZZZ

[Z]<
>/gh/V./3332/1991/1992/#22/

'...everlasting tv new coverage...'
/1888/88/552
'..listen to outpsyjah')/..'
+++++++++++++++++++++

[Z]<
'ZZZZZZZZZZZZZZZ.......'

c:/memory/>mind
++++++++
c:/time
>_my.xxxxxxxxxx
>trance.
>[?]
>[?]
'..zzzzZZZZZZZZZZZZZzzz...'

'trance. ain't nothin', neither's feer...'
'...ZZZZZZZZZZZZZZZZZZZZZZ...'
'where is r.m€.?'
[?]<

```
'this is war..'
########
c:/+++/Lloyd/2000/system/xxxxxxxxxxxxx/experiments/
>time-warps, 0-16

>E-sides=
```
```
+++
c:/++/2000/system/earthbound/statesave/
c:/+++/1999/volcanostones

++

'R?, where have you been?'
c:/batcountry/files/memory/
the blind hits the windowsill, the sound fills my room...
c:/batcountry/project/chi/division/sound/sounds/sets/0-16
>mainframe.system/13/40/2/30
>project/files/memory
```

```
`ahahaha..'
`..ZZZZZZZ....'
`r.m3.is taking his time...
`..ZZZZZZZZZZZZ..'
`we should leave this behind..'
[Z]<
`ahaha...'
>restricted.documents/
>
>
>
>trance.

[ ]
 ^
 Z
 Z
 Z

>source.documents/restricted/
>sleep/dreams/bat.country/
>restricted.source/documents/sleep/dreams
>c:/bat.country/dreams/human.existence/
>portal/messages/extra.dimensional

>trance.

>mainframe.system/human/messages/
>sleep/dreams/restricted/source.

c:/hope/mainframe/system/human/trance
>tools/war/++99/sleep/rebellion/
>dreams/trance/tools/rebellion
>
>

`where is r.m#.?'
`..ZZZZZZ....'
`I don't want to see feer! but he exists, so we could find a job for him,
at least.'
`...ZZZYYXXXZZZZZ...'
++++++++
+++++
++
`uh..'
`oh! it's r.m3o..'
`we could get pizza..'
`ahahaha...!'
++++
+++++++
+++
++++++++++++++++++

————————

[Z]<
`..ZZZZZZZZ.....!'
`he get's so emotional!'
`it's his job.'
`..zzzzz.....?'
`...ZZZZZZZXXXXXXXXXXXZZZZZZZZZZZZZZZZZZZZZ.....'
```

```
>>
>
>

'..sigh..'
'it's probably from tv planet!'
'this is loud..!'

the [Z]< didn't move.

'what does he want?'
'I dunno, he keeps switching off. and on. and off.'
'giving us seizures.'
'we're mostly staring in mirrors...'
'change the channel.'
'please?'
'continue.'
>
>>

c:/gherkin/m/

>
>

>/cowbells/over9000/
>
'ok, sorry,'
'this is out of control!'
'ahaha..'
'ok, so all_meaning exists?'
'what?'

>all.meaning_noodles
>noodles.

>all_meaning/
>>

[Z]<

>all.meaning/files/memory/
>

'we are in bat.country'
'we can't stay here!'

>memory/time/all/meaning
>all/
>

'CHOKO+++'
'+++'

>__all.meaning/files/pictures/
>/0-16/+++/meta.place/++
>

'..ZZZZZZZ....'
'r.m3o?'
'++++....ZZZZ....'
```

```
[Z]< has died.jks

>meta.place/++/bat_country/relax/rebellion/mu/
>0-16/')/+++
>all.meaning/all_meaning/all/meaning/
>pictures/all/bat.country/rebellion/all/meaning/pictures/

'ok, I'm sorry.'
'..zzzzzz...'
'you know place?'
'ZZZZZZZZZZZZZZZZ....'
'this kind of makes sense. he keeps creating static. it's overpowering. and
the console. leads us nowhere.'
'...zzzzZZZZzzzzz...'
'King is going to want to see us again'
'all.meaning could mean nothing.'
'.zzzz...'

[Z]<
+++++++++
++++_++++
++_++++++
++++_++++
+++++_+++

>all.meaning/files/

[Z]<ZZZZZZZZ

+++++++++
'..zzzzzZZZ...'
'there's nothing on t.v. really, there's nothing.'
'skyrises, t.v's, trance.'

>all_meaning/files/
+++

>r.m3o/files
>memory/files/
>CHOKO/++

c:/all.meaning/files/memory/
<memory/files>
>: seizures
>: meaning
>:

'this is pointless.'
++

>trance/files/all/
>')/

>redirect:/trance

>
>
>
```

```
>>
>all_meaning:/hiddenfiles/
:/memory:/

>:Demonemon/
daimon/

>/Delilah/memory/files
>
>
>redirect:hiddenfiles/
/all.meaning/Delilah/
;/home/hiddenfiles/++91/
>

[Z]< is dicking with 1 battery and accidentally ruins it.
'we need another battery.'
'this is one hell of a party!'
'the music is amazing!'
'..zzZZZZZzzzzz....!'
'there was a fire..'
CHOKO++ gets bitten

+++++
+++

>/seizures: allfiles/

'that's too many.'
'why are we so messed up?'
'whose fault is this?'
[Z]<
'..+++++++.....'
'....zzz....'
'r.m3o.. +++'
>seizures:allfiles/memory
>all:meaning/all.meaning/files
+++

XXXXX+++
:/files

++CHOKO,
__r.m3o
'..zzzzzz...'
[Z]< is confused.
'....zzzzzZZZZZZZZzzzzzz....'
++

+++

[Z]<zombiez!!!

...

>>>
>
>
>:all.meaning/memory/files/gh/.V/++91/hidden.documents/directory/hidden_/
```

there were demons in the cameras... they were escaping - people____

___there were walls, fear had crept in

>>:

>>/Z/

is anything going to happen?

we won!! it was totally intense!+++XXXXXXXXxxxxxx ++music was playin' ++
_ XXXXXXxxxXXXXxXXxXXXX+++++_____ *

*transmission_

>>XXXXXxxxxxx <

>>>>>>>>>>>>>>>>>>>>>>>>>>>:terminal_

_____/Z/<_____
_____

<<<<<<<<<<<<<<<<<<<<<<<<:

_codex_433_211.1_ .3_ 42222. _ !222_ ++_monitor## _[hidden.]:
>
>

>
>>>:/*

nothing happens..

...

>>__

```
//:list.index:/monitor//:<<<
>
>
>   100   11    01    0100  10    101   00    10    10    1001  01    0
    101   001   01    00    1001  0     101   01    0     1001  0
    1001  01    01    001   0101              1001  01    00    101   001
    01    0     10    100   101   010   10    10    10    101   0     1
    10    10    10    10    10    10    100   10    100   11    0     11
    0     11    0     11    00    101001      01    00    1010  0     101
    00100 101   0<<<<<<<<<<terminal://freedom.?/file.exit//:list##//:<<<

>oiuw 908   woi   wq    oiuq  3q    oiu3q q     io    3     3poi  3oiu  3qq
      3iouq 3qkj  h3    q987eqq     eoiug qeq   89    qeq   e987  qe
      qeipuh      qe    e98p  ee    qpiuq eeqp98qeeqpiuyq   ee    p98y
      qe98p yeq   ep98y qe
      qe89y<<<<<<<<<<<<<terminal//:freedom./:list.//:<<<<<<<<<<

>list.index//:monitor//:directory/:U52//:7112//:dream.freedom//:<<<<<<<
>
>
>list.file//:##index//:monitor.333//:truth//:tv/[Z]//:<<<<

>
>
>
>????//:file.monitor//mod##??/:list.index//:[Z]<

>//:list.truth//:<
>>terminal://list.index//??#list//:
>
>
>
>file.index//:s26/list.terminal//:reach//<<<<<<<<<<<<<<<<<<<<
/////:list.index//:terminal/monitor.file/:<<<<<<<<<<<<<<
>//.list/:hope//freedom:/index#++//:recover/file/x/monitor//:<<<<<<<<<<<<<<<
<<<<<<
/??.list//:freedom.dream//:index__++//:file.system//:truth.file//:dream.ind
ex<<<<<<<<<<<<<<<<<<
//:file#++//:hope/truth/freedom//:file.monitor/list//:>>>>>>>>>>>>>>>>>>>>>
>>>>>>
>>>>>>>>>>>>>>>>>>>>>>>>>>>>>>>>>>>file.truth//hack#mod++//:x//monitor.file/
/:U52/s26<<<<<<<<<

1    0     101   011   0     101   01    1     0     101   01    0     101
     001   01          11    001010      01    010   0100  01001010    01
     01    0101001010  101   0     1010010101010     0     100100101
     00100101    010   1010  01    00    101001      010   00101010    010
     0010100     01    00001 1     0911  001010      101   01020 00    101
     010100117111      1     89171 1     1     1     0911  111   14321
     11    1     189711      2           28          11
     118711101   18711                   1987  1     2     34
     112         8912              1912        2     2778
     9           90          2           2789  1     1     19    12    87
           2098  2     908   2     2     0     12908       2     98    2
     2     9     2     2<<<<<<<<<<<<
://truth.index//:file.monitor//:list.dream/freedom./:<<<<<<<<<<<<<<<<
>>>>>>>>>>>>>>>>>>>>>>>>>.terminal//:file.monitor//list/dream.file//:truth.i
ndex//:<<<<<<<<<<<
```

[21]

```
>10   00    101   000   100   101   1     001   001   01    001   001   00
      1011  010101      1     1     9811  78611 61    1     346713138
      1398131     09381137961       189731380   3     1091  31    9871  13
      87    1331908133         3987  3113871          3098  33890 13    87
      3     73    3109813131311001       0     101310      110101      10
      101   01    001   <<<
```

```
//:truth/:terminal.index/:<<<<<
>>>>1 101   001   0     1
1     01    000   10    1
01    01    0     101
01    01    00    10    10
1     00    1010
10100100    10001       100   10
010   0     101   0     10
01    00    1000  1001  0
0100  0

0     10    010   00    10
>>>>>list.file//:freedom.index//:97/file.//:
/list.index//:file.key//:index.monitor/<<<<<<<<<<<<<<<<<<<
//list.adelle//:terminal.index//:list.file/:<<<<<<<<

>
>
>
>




>101   001   01    001   001011      09833131    1     1      98713310981 31
       398131        31    39081 30981 31    398131       3
       <<<<<<<<<<<<<terminal./:truth.key//:file.list//:recover/96//:<<<<<<<<
<<<<<<<<<
>>1    001   0     1001  001   001   001   001   0010  10     109811        091
       1     381   3
4      1981  3908  141   4
81141 9184  1498141       4
1      149081            4     2     89311       218   12     13
1      41    198013
       13    13    13    139813      137910381   3908  31<<<<<<<<<<<<
```

```
##//:dream.list//file//332//:
>>dream.system//list/332//?:
>
>
>
>>>>terminal://list.332//:dream.file//truth.//:
truth//:freedom//:dream.system//:monitor.file//:<<<
>>
        108        091   398        10983              1398  13    3      1
        3ioh131311         lkjh313jn313131   73xc  10    vx1793x      13zn3z073
              8307  13xnbx0n    z     109        3873xn0zz         z3io  3nz
        3z09  z37   z     z     09    z          09zn        n90378        38z
        7ccvxsns13  1     nss   11    fg    1337  g379y79     1h3g1iugg
              i3u   g13sg i1u1s gi3g  ixgiu x     x839x       1k13h k3h1  j1
        38    313sx 10876y3113  89    9863  1988913     937181
        191303      7     3<<<<<<<


//file.332//:dream.truth//:list.freedom//:terminal.system//:


>>>>>>>>>>>>terminal.//:list/file/truth//:freedom.index//:<<<<<
```

```
##//:mod.index//:adelle.list//:file/re./:
>>>>>>>>terminal.??/:monitor.file/:
101  001  0    101
1    0    10

01   0
01   001  01
01   01   0001  0

<<<<<<<<<<<<<<<<list.file/recover//:

>>>>>>terminal./file/adelle.??/:##list//:

10   100  1209313   01   3    1kbn13     1jn1kj      1n1   1
     981x
1x   1xu11 1x13iu3x1ib31xiux3h1iuog     1x____++++++    +    ++   +
     +    ++   +++   +            )(*)( #_#   (
     *!)!#798638973238923210981241h12ib421jkb2198+++=00923419083421bkjb12j+
++++_+___+__++_+__++_+++<<<<


//:adelle.index//:directory/re.//list.file//:terminal.console//:<<<<<


>>>>>>>>>>>>>>>>>>>>>>>list.terminal//:console//:mod.list/monitor.index//:
.index//:list/file/system/adelle//:<<<<<<<<<<<<<<<<

>>>>>>>>>>>>>>>terminal./:list.system//:adelle/dream/system.??/:<<<<<<<<<<<
<<

console.monitor__++++//:??//:adelle//:terminal./console.system//:recover/:

monitor//console.list//:system.list/hidden/file/terminal<</list.file??/:<<<
<<<<<<<<<

>>>>>>>>>>>>>>>>>>list.file//:index.system//:dream/list/adelle/recover//:<<
<<<<<<

1010 10   10   10
     10   10   1000  1

01   001  j    1jn1  1    1    1    1    1    1    1

1    1    jnlijwloijw 1ni1  ionw1
ww   1900981whnw 1n1   winw1 iwn1  c
w11  93u098    113998311   31   309u1 3
31
19081381
1    3
1    309811         1908  1439847474  171y  98    1901  1    1    981
     1
     13908t     410981      41   418418409814    1    1
09   1091  81   3908  133   1
1    313098    13
31   90890     0    0    0    991   331
     3098  13        1908  123   13090 1390890    13    133

>>>>>>>file.recover//adelle/list/system.index//:monitor//:<<<<<<
```

```
adelle./file/index//:terminal.mod33##?//:<<<<<<<<<<
>>>199//:[Z]//??run##++-__--++//??&$//:terminal.monitor//:?1337##//:
>>dream.file_8082//:**mod##list.file//:<<<<<<<<<<<
>>>file.church://:run.index//:<terminal.list//:
10101010!0110100  1001  01    01001 0      00010 10    110))1010    00
      1001  01    0
1     0     001   00    10    10010 0      100   10
1     0     1001  01010
1     0
1     0     10    98!*()!*1198      122981      981   98131313798 1
      1813098     182          19
            1098  1         19081918
119028191021890128      109821      098   1290  18          128    12
      12
      192112      29    10    1028  029   1091  0912<<<<<<<<<<
```

```
##adelle//:<<
file_list.//:
>
>




>>>>>>>>100 0      0     0101  01    0
1     0
1     0    1

0     1001  01    0
      11    0001  00    101   001   01
1
1
01    001   0     10
      1
01    0001  0     1
1     0
1     0
      1
1


1     00001
1     01    0     1


>>>>>>>>>>file.list//:outpsyjah


>>>>10      10    1001  01
1
01

01    0
1     01    0     101
01    01    0     11
      1
01    010c01      kwwk1w0     w0    w
01kx1w      kw10k0      1k    ei0ei1      081         1010  3
3
81
30931
0931
1     03830931031
0[9]

>>>>[Z]<<<<<


list.system//:module//:list/terminal//
```

```
>
>
>




>
>
>
>>>>>>010101010   100   10   10    101   01    0100110011  0
1

01    01    0100110    0    1
01    1

10    01    0    110   0
1     01010
      101   0
1     0010010101      11   0    01    0101  01
01    01    1010   0    0101010    001   1    01    0
      101   01
1     0    10    10
      10
1     0    10101  0
      101   0
1     0
1     01
>>>>>list.file//:outpsyjah')/

00101 0     101    00120200    0    01001233i0  0    039303     3      0
      303   k     303k3 030k03x03xk0        30xm         3s0s   3m0   30m3  03
            3ss3  0303sj03j0j3x0sj03x0jx0k        030330030   33    0s003s
      0k3k0 3030k 3303003      03s0kk3s3sj30        v0h3cn        d0nn0 d30sjs
      3003  j03a0ja3      0aj3  0k    0k    c0c0j sx    sj0   3sj30j3n
      3n03s0n      30n    30j0jsx0jx0jj0jv0jv0jxj00xjjc00j0x0jx03      0j3j03
      c3    j0c03 0j3    0j    x0jj0x      03j    03    j     303    3091
      93101383    093    x03    03    x098  2301  393   x     903   u3    0
      3038309x3   9309x  308    3093  930jx39j9    030   9013vj3jv91jc
      1x9j3 0     39xj39j       39j   3     93    39j   093   x     30x  3  x
      0 3x9x      39     x0     93xu3 8903  9x38  9390  03    8093  8      390
      0398  393   98     //
>>>>>>>>.//:system//:trance//:run.mod//:


system://:terminal.monitor//:##mod.//:
```

```
//:freedom.list//:file.dicentra//:monitor_list<<<<
>>>>>>>>>>>>>>>>>>>>>>>>>//:terminal.file//:<<
>>>>>>>>>>>//:◀◀◀//:▲//:dicentra//file.SCN-7112.332//:<<

□://Δ+□<
>>:6112.337-
||./4<<:-VVV//.

◊//.4112.6<
Δ-⊠||.//7++Δ
:ΔSELEC+//.

>//.SCN:Δ+Δ
■+1110.<<

//.>PLAY-//>>.MOD#[symbol.π]||')/.[TRaVeL.CHARM]:???<<./

□://<.LiSt*tHUd*<<[:SKULL:]||:?!!++6.871.//

[Z]<JUNE'14//:

>>>//:SCN-8112.332




')/_____
```

//:freedom.list//:file.dicentra//:monitor_list<<<<
>>>>>>>>>>>>>>>>>>>>>>>>//:terminal.file//:<<
>>>>>>>>>>>//:◀◀//:▲//:dicentra//file.SCN-7112.332//:<<

□://△+□<
>>:6112.337-
||./4<<:-WW//.

◊//.4112.6<
△-▨||.//7++△
:△SELEC+//.

>//.SCN:△+△
■+1110.<<

//.>PLAY-//>>.MOD#[symbol.π]||')/.[TRaVeL.CHARM]:???<<./

□://<.LiSt*tHUd*<<[:SKULL:]||:?!!++6.871.//

[Z]<JUNE'14//:

>>>//:SCN-8112.332

"XXXXXxxxxXXXXXXXXXx+++++*____ *walking aimlessly_ people were falling.
____"
>
>

'playing chess__*on tiny boards,
downhill...>>bat_country//.scale/:_____XXXXXxxxx+++++_____
_____-
"__<<;4KXXXxxx[the rate at which you ...] _z-a"

>>'XXxxx++..the fever, XXxxxX got it____ XXXXXXXXXXXX++++ ___the fever...
what about us? it's not that close - the ball has gone out... ___XXxtwo
sides____ xXXxxxixtion.. _*XXXXxxxare winning... "

*SCN:9007_
:notes - /Z/
   -

[31]

```
//:freedom.list//:file.dicentra//:monitor_list<<<<
>>>>>>>>>>>>>>>>>>>>>>>>>//:terminal.file7/:<<
>>>>>>>>>>>//:◀◀//:▲//:dicentra//file.SCN-7112.332//:<<

□://Δ+□<
>>:6112.337-
||./4<<:-VW//.

◊//.4112.6<
Δ-▨||.//7++Δ
:ΔSELEC+//.

>//.SCN:Δ+Δ
■+1110.<<

//.>PLAY-//>>.MOD#[symbol.π]||')/.[TRaVeL.CHARM]:???<<./

□://<.LiSt*tHUd*<<[:SKULL:]||:?!!++6.871.//

[Z]<JUNE'14//:

>>>//:SCN-8112.332
```

```
SCN_[S]:333__900000_321_100010010101010100100101000101000100010001000100100__33
##____+++_
>>:
>
>
>'XXXxxmericano!!.. "___well, umm - XXXXXXXXXXXXXXXXXXXXXXXXxxxxxxx_____
-ick it long, XXXXXxxxXblood rushing____ must say, 0-0.. "___to come back,
the test__*full on. <<

>
>
>

>> _it has that much room, a skinny XXxxxx___ ++_ i don't reaXXXXxxxxxx

"*GET LOST IN THE MOMENT*____ hey kids! we're looking at our house from
space!! Florida!__
..football, death... *crowd roars* .. have you got what it takes?"


'..played by company, well it is, in the USA - and that's fantastic__here!
__YINGLI SOLXXXXXxxxxxx___ellani takes the corner!!__'

>
>_nil-nil, very off target - Paris have it..."

"time keeps changing, it doesn't stop... i don't know why? like, it is
moving___ XXXxxx++++++++_____-issed it!! It was an
opportunity___on either side, in the minds - Jones.. <<
/^^^^\
|1|11|:

>>>>>>>>>>"some time on the ball, there - challenge!!"




XXXX
XXXX
XXXX




__might have just been deliberate - i'm sure that, with it like that ...<<

____vicarious - the teams struggling to find the finish___ "
_with his reach there - with all that they have on-load"

__to shag? ___*and why half of Britain is still poor -__EE MORE DETAIL* -
4K- *SON___
```

```
scratch//:337_

>
>
```

```
>>>>>>>>>>>>>>>>>>>>>>>>>>>>>>>>>_://scn:xx773_++//:


>>>>>>>>>>>>>>>>>>:
101    0     103-13       -      1-31  221021
>>>>>>>>>>>>>>>>>:
        123    133   1_
>>>_



>>>>>>>>>>>>       98761 9081  109    3_



>>>>>>>>>>>>>>>>:[%//:_missing]
```

```
SCN_XY_++

>>:/_##9(11992093399011933910010010    0      1011
        10    1
01      0
        10
1       0
0
1
100     1
01
01
01
010
1
01
01
0       10
1
0       1
01
01
0
01      0             101    01     0
1
1             101    01     00     101
1
        10    1
0
1
01            1      01     0      101    01     0      100    1
01      1
01
01
01      1     <<<<<<<<<<<<<<<<<<<<<<<<<<<<<<<<<<<<:/Z/[z-z
```

SCNXY_773_<<<<

>>##list.dream/_337/#dream/???+++/Z/[z-z:<<<

>>>//:

SCNXY_774_<<<<

>>the galaxy. _full.list##//:_ seeking all meaning and endless
sourceXXXXXXXXXXXXX that could
potenialXXXXXXXXXXXXXXXXXXXXXXXXXXXXXXXXXXXXXXXXXall humanity_
xxxxXXXXXXXXXXX_ without any real reason_ xxxxxXXXXXXXXX_xxxXXxxxxxfunk_
and the desire_ spaceXXXXXXX_ .XY

<<<<<<<<<<<<<<<<<<<<<<<<<<<<<<<<<<<<<<<<<<<<<<<<<<

_res.774

what? _file.XXXXXXXXXX...

_do we need to change time? XXXXXXXXXXX_is it
possible?++++++++###################XXXXXX_

.list<<<

>>>//:

```
SCNXY_**+___+**_

>>>_333___+39_heine//:333 1-  11    1 -1  _01001      10    1
1     0     10
1     00    1
      10
      1     10
      10


1     0
1                    1 010
1        0   1
         1
10    1
 1    01

         1      <<<<<<<<<<<<
```

```
dicentra.codex//:mod##
>>>>>>>>>>>>>
//.list:terminal//:monitor.file//:<<<<<<<<<<<<
//:▲//:portal//:yin//:heine/adelle_index//:monitor.list//:<<<<<<<<<<<
>>>>>>>>>>>>>>>>>>>>>>>>
>>>>>>>>>>>>>>>>>>>>>>>>
```

```
>>/:[warning!]:[hidden.files]//:Dicentra_')/.breed||HWKU52<<
                              >[symbolοπ]//.++'JUNE'14

>>>[Z]
[Z]<<')/.Ver.1.2
||')/.breed|HWKU52
||Ver_1.1[symbol.π]
>
>
>
<9311SCN:[Z]')/.||[symbolοπ]//.++-o//')/.||o-||')/.||[symbolοπ]++//.6-
14'<<-
o//:

[symbolοπ]||')/.++//:
>
>>

[WARNING:]<<<<<<<<<<<<<<<<<<<<<<<<<<<<<<//:terminal
□
□
▽
+
+
□
-
-
▷
|
SCN-7112.332
        ..
>>>>>>>>>>>>>>>>>>>>>>>>>>>>>>[warning.]<<<system.file//:mod##hack//:freedo
m_Dicentra/list.file//:monitor_
>>>>>>>>>>>>>>>>>>>system.log//:##$$??//:>>>
```

```
//.list:freedom<<<
10     001   0101001     0      101    01
1      0     100   1
       1
0      1
0      101   00    10    1
001
0      10    10
0
1
0
0101
0
1
0100  1
01    0
1
010
0
1
00
1
0
10
1
01
001   0
010   1001  00    10101 01     0101  <<<<<<<<<<<<<<<<<<
>>//redirect.terminal//:monitor.file//:z/x/dicentra//:<<<
>>>>>>codex//:file/<
//:dream.freedom/terminal//:dicentra//:yin>>>>>>>>>>>>>>>>>>>>>>>>>>>>>>>
>>>>>>>>>>>>>>>>>>>>>>>>>>>>>
>>>>>>>>>>>>>>>>>>>>>>>>>
>>>>>>>>>>>>>>>>>>>>>>
>>>>>>>>>>>>>>>>>>
>>>>>>>>>>>>>>>
>>>>>>>>>>>>
>>>>>>>>
>
list.truth//:dream.file//:system.freedom//:<<<<<<<<<<<<<<<<<<<<<<<<<<<<<<<<
```

```
//all_meaning//:file/precis//:
/file.list//:index.terminal//:console/*/:
>>>111      1      00     10     1
     01     0      100
1      1      0      1
01            1
01     0101   1      1      01
1      01     01
01     01     01     01     01     0      101    01     0      11            1      1
       11            101    01     01     01     01     0      10     11     0      11
       01     0      101    01     01     0      1001   1      0
```

file//:terminal.precis//:monitor.file/list//mod*++//<<<<<<<<<<<<<<<<<<<<<<<<<
<<<<<<

>>>file.destiny/file/precis.file//:terminal.mod/monitor.index//:<<<<<<<<<

```
//heine.delilah//:index.file//:<<<<<<<<<
>
>
>
>//:nature.file//:dream.index/:<<<
>10100101011          00    1000  100   1000  11    1     098   11    33
      11    3709131    380913     13908
      1<<<<<<<<<<<<//terminal./list//:<<<<<<
>>>>>>>>>>>>file.delilah//:list/file/index./nature//:<<<<<


>
>1    101    098    11    33701891           19181331    1908  11    3890131
      3908  131   3908  13    139098         13    19381 31    3098131
      37821120982424098311    0     198   3139081      31
      <<<<<<<<<<<<<<<<<<<<<<<<<<<<<<<<<<terminal.//:list.file//:heine.inde
x/<<
>list.index//:monitor.file//<<<<<<<<<<<<<<<<<<<<<<<
```

```
>>//:file/directory//:heine//:delilah//
##file.//:
.>>system<<:
++//??:file.//system:
__system.//:file.//directory/:retrieve//:memory/file./system//:
//:delilah//<<:j:ig//:re/file.//:
<<system.<<//:>>
//:heine//:system./directory//:
>>>>>>>>>>>
>>>>>>>:10010010101001001     0010  00    10010010     00100
      101001        0     0
              110    01110 0
1    0


1         101101
      111                      100101      10100101001 01    0010  1
         1
1         11

1                    11    0101010    01    00100       010100       01
      1
         101010      010   00    10    0    100001011010      00     0
      0101  0     0     10100 0100100     01010010100 0     100010
      0100100101
1     0    1         1001010     01010 00100 00    010   0101010     00
      010   010   0101010      00    101010      00    010   00    10010100
      0101  0101010
      1010100      0     010   00100 0     0     00100100     0     0101010
      0101  010   0010101     00010 01    01    00    010
1


         1010  0     101
1
         10    010   10
0
      1010
10


1
0         0101  00    101   0     10    1

101

10


      1
1     1
1
      0     0     101   01001 0     10    00    010   00101
      110   0010101
1
>>>>>>>>>>>>>>>>100101010101>>>>>>10010101010,<<<<<<11

file.?/:system:/:heine//:re/directory//:<<
```

```
//:truth.key/:monitor.file/<<<<
>truth.file/map//:key.index//:monitor.list<<<<<
>>>>>>>terminal.code//:list.key//:>>>
>1      0     100   1000101    00    10    100   100   100   10100 11      098
        12    12789621    1      09812 129812      1261356135  613987        2
        389   13    2837060     9908  712   1308746     61851271806 313
        0987218746   469279     813789613   66    1807  16311 0912  130998
        713   07    3-    9-8173      1987137     137987      13
        13970389767 88130 1738  13671 379887      13    319877      13
        38704216166 17    127788      901721827   128   61441671262178    13
              89237329837537532 9879  2349        +++++_____
        09872384782398239298   98    98234783    34++++_____
>>>>>>>>key.code//:list.monitor_/:terminal.file/>terminal.code//:list.index
/file/code/key/list//:
>freedom:/dream<<://{??}|://?/_cell.//:monitor.file/index//:<<<<
>>^^^^^^^^6666666666***666666666666666666666666666666666666666666666666666__
___---+++==??//:"##!!*^^6//:
1      1098  13130981    31    3     180913      13098 31    1398908913098
       1     1313908193831      098131      3098908     13    1398  13098
       19081 313980      13    13981 31    839081      3     13980 13
       1098811     309813      09813980313897   47417 y130938      13
       2373820     987   42422424vbu42242490871       0982249087   24
       24897 2     2oi4h 2498  24    24ih2 b     242   879   2492  487   24-
982    20981 14    987   244278690   13    98    1     13987 2429872
       248972947824 6     9872  98    42h   24hu  oi429 24    987
       4987  29874 987   982   29    2     2     0     674202      4988924
       724-  47    98724870     6274726     6     4++++ _____-----
09878798897 179849874      18397131789 1390813798     1379813008731    1
       37018311380 7136131    871298711487613784613   13987 13    187
       1398713<<<<<<<<<<<<terminal.list//:key.list//:code.file//.list_monito
r/index.key//:<<<<<<<<<
>>>>>>>>>>>.file//_klkl//KLKL||_:^^??://:##:##~\:??/++<<<<<:
```

[45]

```
//:truth.key/:monitor.file/<<<<
>truth.file/map//:key.index//:monitor.list<<<<<
>>>>>>>terminal.code//:list.key//:>>>
>1     0     100   1000101    00    10   100    100   100   10100 11      098
       12    12789621    1      09812 129812        1261356135  613987       2
       389   13    2837060     9908  712   1308746      61851271806 313
       0987218746  469279      813789613    66    1807  16311 0912  130998
       713   07    3-    9-8173       1987137       137987       13
       13970389767 88130 1738  13671 379887       13    319877       13
       38704216166 17    127788       901721827    128   61441671262178      13
                   89237329837537532 9879  2349          +++++_____
             09872384782398239298    98    98234783     34++++_____
>>>>>>>>key.code//:list.monitor_/:terminal.file/>terminal.code//:list.index
/file/code/key/list//:
>freedom/dream/cell//:monitor.file/index//:<<<<
>>     1     1098  13130981    31    3     180913       13098 31
       1398908913098     1     1313908193831       098131       3098908       13
       1398  13098 19081 313980       13    13981 31    839081       3
       13980 13    1098811      309813      09813980313897      47417 y130938
       13    2373820      987   42422424vbu42242490871
       0982249087   24    24897 2     2oi4h 2498  24    24ih2 b      242   879
       2492  487   24-982       20981 14    987   244278690   13    98    1
       13987 2429872      248972947824    6     9872  98    42h   24hu
       oi429 24    987   4987  29874 987   982   29    2     2     0
       674202      4988924      724-  47    98724870      6274726      6
       4++++ _____-----09878798897    179849874    18397131789 1390813798
       1379813008731     1     37018311380 7136131       871298711487613784613
       13987 13    187
       1398713<<<<<<<<<<<<terminal.list//:key.list//:code.file//.list_monito
r/index.key//:<<<<<<<<<
```

```
__+//:file.list/index//:terminal.mod//:
>>bat.country//:list/file/depository/x//:
        10              10    01
        101   010   0     1     10
1       10    10
        10    1
10      10    101   0
        11    01    01    0
        10    10    1
01            10
1
0       110
        1
0       1
0       10    10
1
01
0       1
1


>>>>>>>>>>>>>>>terminal.mod//:index//:
monitor.list//:portal/file/x://
portal://list.terminal//:
list.directory//file/portal/terminal/mod##/:
??//terminal:/list.mod//:index.file<<<

        11    0
1       01    01
010     101
01      01    01    0     1
01      01    01
0       1     0     1
0       10
        10    10
        10    1
1       0     100   10
        10    101   00    10    1
00
0
1010    10    100   11
01      0
1
01      0
1       0

>>>>thought//:monitor//list.index//:church.mod##//:
list.terminal//portal//index/file/z//:<<<<<<
>>>>>[Z]://file/depository.list//portal.terminal//:<<<<<<<<<<<<

1010101    101         11    01010 01    001
```

```
##exit//:terminal./file.directory//:
>>>>>>
>
>>>
>
>


>
>



>>>>terminal./file_corrupt++??/:
>>[terminal.]//:file.corrupt??/:
+++___[terminal:]//:file.memory//:
>>>
>
>
>


>>>terminal//:?
>>//:[retrieve]://
>>>>>000100010001000100000100010010001000010001000001001001010010010000101010010
100
>>>>

>
>
>100010
>
>111001
>
>//:??//:
>>00100100101001001101??//:
c:/terminal.??//:
terminal.mod//:
retrieve//:
terminal.//:mod//recover://:
terminal.mod//:
retrieve//:
>>>>>>>>
>>mod://recover://:
>
>


>
>mod://:00100010100010001010001001010010000100010000100110000
>1001000100010000100010000
>11000001000010000010010001001001010100
>1__++00101000100001010



>0101
>0010001001001
>1001001000010100///
01001000010001010
01001
```

```
001000100000000000000//////??????/////11_100001
100100100100100101_++1000101////??
>mod://:###/recover//:
>001010000010010
10001000100001000001000010010010001
10011111111111111111111
>>>>>>>>

>terminal.console//file/memory<
<<<<<<<<<<<<
000   100100101
0    00    00    022222
              200200202   00202002011
1010101101  001010100   10100101
11200020100012   010   0
100020020   00


                 0200200101001200210
120021
01
10   0

110x11x1
0
010   1      zzz00101010 10100010101
1010010000
01z0x00100100100w00000010    01010 0010100
10100
10   110101               010100     0      0
1010

10101010    0     0     o1001i10100w0wx0010z10
1000z0x0100100   010   0     0000  01i1101
010        u__+++      0010011    10010 01001
>>terminal.//file.directory//:
##memory//:mod/
>>terminal://
[terminal.]://:mod/:
>
>
>
>
>100010100100
>10010010000100100      0100  02010010
0010k10ks00101000x0x0z010010  0101001x
>11001010x0010001z01x0100      01x0x10z11100x01x
>0100x01z010x010zo1z0i1010z00z01    1z    z0
>100  0    0010z010x010     1w0   0s
>1010010://:1---1-      --_____+++++++
###__++
>>>>
--mod://:
>mod/:_failure.system/file.directory//:
mod##exit//:_failure://system:/redirect:/
>>terminal.//files:[system.]//:
mod//:
>>>>mod//:console.//:
```

```
##110100001000100101001001010010
!#00101001
#0010010001010
>>>>>>1010010
---101001---101--10      -01001-100
__=++++
//__-1001010001001010____+++
??;////:
>>>>>>>.101010010010010100://:
??//:delilah//adelle//:
//:system//:
mod??//:##
system.mod//:
boot.file/:
.system//:
file/:mod//:system.retrieve//:boot.file//:??
//:<<system_file.terminal//:boot.file//:??
//:retrieve|:
>>>>>>>>>>>>
>>>>>101001001000101001
001010001001010:100100010//??
//:adelle/file./directory//:
??//:
0010100010100010//:
>>.console//:terminal//:mod/console./terminal./mod//:adelle//:
>>>>file.//:mod##00100010010001000//:
>//:101010001000100101
>
>


>
>
0101010//://??
!Xz!xzzz1xxx1zz1z10010101xx0xioz0//:
>>>>>>mod.file//:11000//:file./system//:
>
>
>
#mod//:file<<.terminal//:console//:exit##
```

```
>>list.file//:list/data//:key//:9123<<<<<<<<<<<<<<
>>>>> 10     10     101    -39    19     13901 3      13789 1368   3
       13    1687   113907        13     189713
       13    9873   13987 13
39     7318   1387   138
1      13     1389731098  13
>>>>>>>>>>>>>>>>>.terminal//:list.monitor//:system//:mod##hack<<<<<<<<<

       13098120984 1382   121
       24    910    8      13
       13    1098   3      1
3      1930   13
       >>>>>>>>>>>>>>>>>>>>>>>>>>>>>list.monitor//:dream.list/freedom##/:13
       0183
13     1983
13     1089  1
1      38
       01893.<<<<<<<<<<
```

```
exit??//:##
//;file?:/:
>>>>>>>101001
0100101
1
01001001
1
01
0
010

000100
10
      0      0
      0
      20    020   0     0      )
      0

)      0
@
))00@0      0@)    )00

0)0   )0)   )@

))202
20200s000w0
0     0))   w0    w

001000      0110
110
      00    01    0     10010
0     0
1     0
1
001
010
100100x100x
      10100
10
      1000
1
001
00
010
0100
10
01    0
0101001
0
1
0     10
010
      10

01000001010
0

0
0

00001
```

```
0
        001    01     0       0      01
                1
0010
        1
0
0       0      0
0
        0
0       0
                       0
        0
1

        0


10                     0


1       0      1
0

        1


        1
        1
1
>>>>
>
>
>file//:directory//:
>file//:terminal.exit//:
```

```
##??/:terminal.monitor//:index//:
/file.list//:
>
>




>
>
```

```
>
>>>>>01000101010://:file.directory//:index.file//:
>>terminal://monitor.index//:
0101   01    1      0
       101   01
1      1
01
       1001
1      0
       1101  01     0
       1
011    0
1
11     0
1
1      010   10     10
       1
01     1
0      1
0      11    1      01
       101   1      0
       11
       101   01
1
1      01    01     01
0
>>>
>monitor//:U52/file.list//:
>
>
```

```
//:file.directory//:adelle>>
01    0    101
      101  0    1
1     0    10   1
0     1
1
0     1010 1    0
      1
      101  0    10
1     0    10
      101  0
      1
>>>>file.index//:terminal//x/
//:thought/x/file.list<<
monitor./:mod##//:adelle/x/file.list/
##freedom/x//:monitor.terminal//:file/list/x
//100 01   0    101  //:
##church//:file.list/terminal.mod//:index/
list/:file.list//:x/<<
>>dream.list//:file.mod//#
<<<<<<<<<<<<<<<<<<<<<<<<<<<<011    01    01    01    01    01
101  0    101  01
1    0    101  01
01   01   01   0101 01   0
     101  1
11   0
01   1    0    1010
11   0
     1         101  0101 01
01   1    0101 01   010       101  01
10   1    0    1    01   1010 111  0011 01   01

>>>>>>>>>>>>>>......dream.list//:##mod//:adelle.mod//terminal.list//:
/x/file.list/:depository//:
list.index//:mod//:
mod##//:
index.list//:file.mod//##list//:
>>>
>10101     10   09   18   97y  1vu  hv171g     1          19871
    h1kij h1   189h1h    1uh1jk1    b    1b98 1h89 18   91
    1h98  1h   1kjvx1    1hxy 1x    1a1a15543av 1jhv1    1vj
    mbss  1iy1sc1   hgc1 1s981 0981 4361 8    10981     1hsiuha
    b          uia  1uba1 1g1  u    1    8791      198zzgh9h  1z8
    181   18u1 98h1      871       178  11   817198     1    1
    19711 yh1  97y1 1    y9   171       y9   1    191  71y1 91
          191  79   11y  171  9811 y1   9    8    17   1171179
    1     981y 198y1 9y1 189y119y1  981  981  1iuh1     1h91
    hzvxiu     18   1z9zu 198uzzh    i1uzh 1h89zh1z  11   uhaihxih1
    iuh1  981  ah1  ajkaa 198a1 ha1ziuhaaa iuh1ah     1iua1 ai1u1
    aha1<<<<<<<<<<<<<<<<

>mod//:index/file/x//:terminal.index//:file/x/:
//:freedom/file/:depository//:<<<<
```

```
##monitor.//:
console.mod//:
terminal>>/:monitor
>>
>


>
>
>>>>>10100100010010:/
10001010010>>monitor##.?/:
>>



>>
>>




>
>
>
>        >        >        >100100010001001
0010
monitor//:console.
>>//:heine:/:mod##//:
console//:monitor./:system/re/directory//:
//:monitor//:mod
##>>>>>>10010100100100100101001010
>>>>>10010010101001
0010010000   0010   01010  01
      0001010      001010      0100  010   0
      0101010
            002100100
>>>>>>>>>>>>>>>>>>>>>>>>.......

console.mod//:>>system//:re/mod://:
monitor.mod//:>>mod/system/re/directory//:
monitor.mod//:file/system.//:

>>
>>
>


>>>>>00101000101001010100100101001001>>>>monitor.//:console//:
>>mod//:


//monitor//:mod//:



>>>
>
>
>
```

```
>
                         1001001
10010        1010   0101  10010 01001010     1010
11010 0101   010100       01001 01010 10001 01001
>>>>>>>>>>
monitor//:system
//mod??/:
##mod//:
main.frame//:mod//:monitor//:
system//:
re/delivery/frame/file/:monitor//:mod??//:##mod//:
1001010      10    01    0      00100101
      001    0     01010

010    010    010           0101
       10     010    010100
1
       010
1
0      010
10
       >><>
<<>>010010010       010101

//:monitor//:main.frame//:mod//:
>>>>>0101010001
010101
10001

1001
0110
0
       10    1
0      10
0
              0
0
1      010101
10010
1
0
0010101               0
0      1
0      1
0
                      0
       10
10


01001
010010011
       1     10    1000  010    00010 01

00
       1
0
001
01     00    10
1
0      1
```

[57]

```
000
01
00
                    0      0110

0       010   1
100
        1
00
00    1
0

        10
0     0
00
```

main.frame//:system//:mod.//:monitor//system.mod//:
file./mod>>system/mod./file/directory/re/delivery/<<<

>>10010101001<<<
system.file>>main/frame.mod//:
<<<<010010001000101001000100 0
0100 001   0
0   1
00100

        00
0
0   0   101
00
        1001   101   0101 0

10   101
0   10   01010

010   100   010
        0
10010
01010
                    01010

0   01010
        0
1011   1010 1   0   101   00   10   1
0
01   010   100   1
0   1
1

0   10   10
10
        1
000
1   0010 10
1
0   1
0
              0   10   1
0   1
        1
```
```

```
00    1
      1
0     1
00    1              10    1
<<<<<<<<<<<<<<<<<<<<<<<main.frame/mod//:
system//hack##//:mod//monitor//:file//mod:
//system//:terminal./mod://:
hack##monitor.mod//:terminal./mod//:
monitor##mod.//:
terminal//:system//:file//
re/directory//:mod//:hack##$##$//:$$$//:
mod.//:monitor//:hack//$$###//:
++++_____monitor//:hack##/:mod//:
>>>>>>>>
>>>>
>>>




>
>
>
>
>1010000    0010  0100  0010  100   1001
10010
1011  1      0     10    100   1010
      1      1     100
      101


1     10     10    1
      10
      11
0     11     1           101   010   1
      10     1
      10     1
      10     11    1           10    101   0     1     0     1
      1
      1
0     10     10    1
0     1      010   1
      1
      11           10    11    001   10    1
1     1
      10
      101
01    0
>>>>>>>>>monitor.terminal//:mod//:console.hack##//:monitor//
.>
>
>
>
>
>
>
>
```

//:freedom//:mod//:hack##<<<<<

```
##monitor.//:
console.mod//:
terminal>>/:monitor
>>
>


>
>
>>>>>10100100010010:/
10001010010>>monitor##.?/:
>>



>>
>>



>
>
>
>      >     >      >100100010001001
0010
monitor//:console.
>>//:heine:/:mod##//:
console//:monitor./:system/re/directory//:
//:monitor//:mod
##>>>>>>10010100100100100101001010
>>>>>10010010101001
0010010000  0010  01010 01
      0001010      001010      0100  010   0
      0101010
            002100100
>>>>>>>>>>>>>>>>>>>>>>>>>.......

console.mod//:>>system//:re/mod://:
monitor.mod//:>>mod/system/re/directory//:
monitor.mod//:file/system.//:

>>
>>
>


>>>>>00101000101001010100100101001001>>>>monitor.//:console//:
>>mod//:


//monitor//:mod//:



>>>
>
>
>
```

```
>
                     1001001
10010       1010  0101  10010 01001010    1010
11010 0101  010100       01001 01010 10001 01001
>>>>>>>>>
monitor//:system
//mod??/:
##mod//:
main.frame//:mod//:monitor//:
system//:
re/delivery/frame/file:monitor//:mod??//:##mod//:
1001010      10    01    0      00100101
      001    0     01010

010    010   010           0101
       10    010   010100
1
       010
1
0      010
10
       >><>
<<>>010010010      010101

//:monitor//:main.frame//:mod//:
>>>>>0101010001
010101
10001

1001
0110
0
       10    1
0      10
0
       0
0
1      010101
10010
1
0
0010101           0
0      1
0      1
0
           0
       10
10


01001
010010011
       1    10    1000    010    00010 01

00
       1
0
001
01     00    10
1
0      1
```
[62]

```
000
01
00
                        0       0110

0       010     1
100
        1
00
00      1
0

        10
0       0
00
```

main.frame//:system//:mod.//:monitor//system.mod//:
file./mod>>system/mod./file/directory/re/delivery/<<<

>>10010101001<<<
system.file>>main/frame.mod//:
<<<<01001000100010010001000
0100   001   0
0   1
00100
.
        00
0
0   0   101
00
        1001   101   0101   0

10   101
0   10   01010

010   100   010
                0
10010
01010
                        01010

0   01010
                0
1011   1010   1   0   101   00   10   1
0
01   010   100   1
0   1
1

0   10   10
10
        1
000
1   0010   10
1
0   1
0
                0   10   1
0   1
        1
```
```

```
00    1
      1
0     1
00    1           10    1
<<<<<<<<<<<<<<<<<<<<<<main.frame/mod//:
system//hack##//:mod//monitor//:file//mod:
//system//:terminal./mod://:
hack##monitor.mod//:terminal./mod//:
monitor##mod.//:
terminal//:system//:file//
re/directory//:mod//:hack##$##$//:$$$//:
mod.//:monitor//:hack//$$###//:
++++_____monitor//:hack##/:mod//:
>>>>>>>>
>>>>
>>>
```

```
>
>
>
>
>1010000    0010  0100  0010  100   1001
10010
1011  1     0     10    100   1010
      1     1     100
      101

1     10    10    1
      10
      11
0     11    1           101   010   1
      10    1
      10    1
      10    11    1           10    101   0     1     0     1
      1
      1
0     10    10    1
0     1     010   1
      1
      11          10    11    001   10    1
1     1
      10
      101
01    0
>>>>>>>>>monitor.terminal//:mod//:console.hack##//:monitor//
.>
>
>
>
>
>
>
```

//:freedom//:mod//:hack##<<<<<

```
##monitor.//:
console.mod//:
terminal>>/:monitor
>>
>


>
>
>>>>>10100100010010:/
10001010010>>monitor##.?/:
>>



>>
>>




>
>
>
>       >       >       >100100010001001
0010
monitor//:console.
>>//:heine:/:mod##//:
console//:monitor./:system/re/directory//:
//:monitor//:mod
##>>>>>>100101001001001001101001010
>>>>>10010010101001
0010010000  0010  01010 01
      0001010      001010      0100  010   0
      0101010
              002100100
>>>>>>>>>>>>>>>>>>>>>>>>>>.......

console.mod//:>>system//:re/mod://:
monitor.mod//:>>mod/system/re/directory//:
monitor.mod//:file/system.//:

>>
>>
>


>>>>>0010100010100101010100100101001001>>>>monitor.//:console//:
>>mod//:


//monitor//:mod//:



>>>
>
>
>
```

```
>
                            1001001
10010        1010   0101   10010 01001010     1010
11010 0101  010100         01001 01010 10001 01001
>>>>>>>>>>
monitor//:system
//mod??/:
##mod//:
main.frame//:mod//:monitor//:
system//:
re/delivery/frame/file/:monitor//:mod??//:##mod//:
1001010     10    01    0       00100101
      001   0     01010

010   010   010          0101
      10    010   010100
1
      010
1
0     010
10
      >><>
<<>>010010010     010101

//:monitor//:main.frame//:mod//:
>>>>>0101010001
010101
10001

1001
0110
0
      10    1
0     10
0
      0
0
1     010101
10010
1
0
0010101          0
0     1
0     1
0
            0
      10
10


01001
010010011
      1     10    1000   010    00010 01

00
      1
0
001
01    00    10
1
0     1
```

```
000
01
00
                0       0110

0       010   1
100
        1
00
00    1
0

        10
0       0
00
```

main.frame//:system//:mod.//:monitor//system.mod//:
file./mod>>system/mod./file/directory/re/delivery/<<<

>>10010101001<<<
system.file>>main/frame.mod//:
<<<<010010001000101001000100 0
0100   001   0
0   1
00100

        00
0
0   0   101
00
        1001   101   0101   0

10   101
0   10   01010

010   100   010
        0
10010
01010
                        01010

0   01010
        0
1011   1010   1   0   101   00   10   1
0
01   010   100   1
0   1
1

0   10   10
10
        1
000
1   0010   10
1
0   1
0
                0   10   1
0   1
        1
```
```

```
00    1
      1
0     1
00    1              10    1
<<<<<<<<<<<<<<<<<<<<<main.frame/mod//:
system//hack##//:mod//monitor//:file//mod:
//system//:terminal./mod://:
hack##monitor.mod//:terminal./mod//:
monitor##mod.//:
terminal//:system//:file//
re/directory//:mod//:hack##$##$//:$$$//:
mod.//:monitor//:hack//$$###//:
++++_____monitor//:hack##/:mod//:
>>>>>>>>
>>>>
>>>




>
>
>
>
>1010000    0010  0100  0010  100   1001
10010
1011  1     0     10    100   1010
      1     1     100
      101

1     10    10    1
      10
      11
0     11    1           101   010   1
      10    1
      10    1
      10    11    1           10    101   0     1     0     1
      1
      1
0     10    10    1
0     1     010   1
      1
      11          10    11    001   10    1
1     1
      10
      101
01    0
>>>>>>>>>>monitor.terminal//:mod//:console.hack##//:monitor//
.>
>
>
>
>
>
>
>
```

//:freedom//:mod//:hack##<<<<<

//:<BLU33F//mod#33//')/:

```
CVE-2014-0160
CVE, CVE-2014-0346
>>RFC6520_
NCSC-FI case# 788210
_Q-CERT:file_list

>
>     10    0     10030310   10   1     0     10          13   10
      1001  30    10   1300   1    1310  130   131   398   1398 1     147
      1     1938  13876 1          138080      138   109   1##?_

//:X.509.BYPASS_

_++#  1001  0     1011  0100  00   10    10    100   010   10    1>>>>>>
```

```
CVE-2014-0160
CVE, CVE-2014-0346
>>RFC6520_
NCSC-FI case# 788210
_Q-CERT:file_list

>
>    10    0     10030310    10    1      0      10              13    10
     1001  30    10    1300  1     1310   130    131    398      1398  1     147
     1     1938  13876 1           138080        138    109      1##?_

//:X.509.BYPASS_

_++#  1001  0     1011  0100  00    10    10    100    010    10    1>>>>>>
```

[index_state#0000000001310011111-]:

>
>"fluct_files had been accessed and the present state of index was
persisting beyond our predictions. all_meaning was experiencing a number of
file crashes on a base level - time was disintegrating, so much so that the
city of Face experienced a severe front of blackholes forming on its
Western outer. [Z] was in Face at the time, and linked the index state to a
series of crashes in time that had occurred months earlier to the south of
the city. The holes were patched and a number of save_states were
recovered. The index_ files were allowed to re_file and all_meaning updated
accordingly. [Z] had arranged a meeting with_____

_____being left in time only gave [Z] greater cause to undermine the
leap - or at least, attempt to keep his past."

```
>>>/file.list/<<://tech/list//syntax/4223//:<<
>terminal./file.system:<
>>mod##0987//file.church/<:
list.ruins//:<<<<<<<<<<<<<<<<<<<<<<<<<<<<<<

>>>>>>>>>>>>>>>>>>>>>>>0987//:<
ruins.file/terminal.[hidden]<<
>>>>>>>>>>>>>>>.monitor/list./
church.system//:4332.4223.3442
>>>>>>>>>>>>>>>>>>>>>>>>>.4332
>>>>>>>>>>>>>>>>>332.4223.4332
syntax.file/list//:2.4223.4332
>>>>>>>>>>>>>>>>>>>>>>>>>>>>./
>>>>>>[hidden.]<<<<<<<<<3.3442
>>>>>>>>>>>>>>>>>>>>>>>>>>>//:<
//:[file.missing]()./:223.0987
.//:<<<<<<<<<<<<<<<<<<<<<<<<<

>>>>>>>>>>>>>>>>>>>>>>>>>>>>>/file.list/<<://tech/list//syntax/4223//:<<
>terminal./file.system:<
>>mod##0987//file.church/<:
list.ruins//:<<<<<<<<<<<<<<<<<<<<<<<<<<<<<<

>ruins./terminal.console./:monitor.system//:


<<<<<<<<<<<<<<<<<<<<<<<<<<<<<<<<<<<<<<<<<<<<<
1010   1001  01    010101           101  10101 01    01    01    1      1
       010   1001  001   01    00    10001001   0      0001  000100
       10928212    1     289101216781             10981        1761  765
       1189731     09812098187 6     876   1361387112786       1215  22
       5781  278                     8913731098211267       87              987
       1313091     2     1     3987  3.//ruins.index/:list.file<<

0      1

01     0

1      01    0     101

101

1      001   0

1      10

1


1      101   01    0     1

1

1      0     1

1
```

```
>>>>//:list/file/s/re./[Z]/directory.system//:
```

```
>>>/file.list/<<://tech/list//syntax/4223//:<<
>terminal./file.system:<
>>mod##0987//file.church/<:
list.ruins//:<<<<<<<<<<<<<<<<<<<<<<<<<<<<<<<<

>>>>>>>>>>>>>>>>>>>>>>>>0987//:<
ruins.file/terminal.[hidden]<<
>>>>>>>>>>>>>>>.monitor/list./
church.system//:4332.4223.3442
>>>>>>>>>>>>>>>>>>>>>>>>>.4332
>>>>>>>>>>>>>>>>>>>332.4223.4332
syntax.file/list//:2.4223.4332
>>>>>>>>>>>>>>>>>>>>>>>>>>>>./
>>>>>>[hidden.]<<<<<<<<<3.3442
>>>>>>>>>>>>>>>>>>>>>>>>>>>>//:<
//:[file.missing]().//:223.0987
.//:<<<<<<<<<<<<<<<<<<<<<<<<<

>>>>>>>>>>>>>>>>>>>>>>>>>>>>>>/file.list/<<://tech/list//syntax/4223//:<<
>terminal./file.system:<
>>mod##0987//file.church/<:
list.ruins//:<<<<<<<<<<<<<<<<<<<<<<<<<<<<<<<<

>ruins_/terminal.console./:monitor+system//:


<<<<<<<<<<<<<<<<<<<<<<<<<<<<<<<<<<<<<<<<<<<<<

1010   1001  01    010101          101   10101 01    01    01    1     1
       010   1001  001   01    00   10001001   0     0001  000100
       10928212    1     289101216781          10981        1761  765
       1189731     09812098187 6     876   1361387112786    1215  22
       5781  278                     8913731098211267        87         987
       1313091     2     1     3987  3.//ruins.index/:list_file<<

0    1

01   0

1    01    0    101

101

1    001   0

1    10

1


1    101   01    0     1

1

1    0     1

1
```

```
>>>>//:list/file/s/re./[Z]/directory_system//:
```

all_meaning >> ruins.mod

>
> ____##fail_safe://_mod##3_++/:

>
>##3_ruins.mod//:

_____all_meaning is operational: fluct. index is approx; 3333443433_343-
34433444333.433.43.324.24.34.2332.3.423423423432_322342323.2.3.42.324024990
69369696320_**77878374873282387428282734090090293093200439902409092942 3__--
23429384982934828948229249-23498-2342-839-294829823-94-92-9239-49-29394929-
4882-3-2399492982394-2398-2-9829-394-99293949223-4929-3_   90   8
      909   90   98   90   9   90   9   98   909   09829049   892
      9   29092389039 839   0   9090 930   9292 09382 837   923
      8736 28   36   8   366   287 22897 2   39   8389 327382
            8297328   233   27932 877   2328787   23   238978
      2389723   8   3   3   327862   32   389778   322
      872   89723 %%//:

##fluct.index_

>>bat.country//:mod##index_fluct

_____join bat.country today!!___air-quest is taking applications!___

```
bat.country//:_lydia_senate:8082

>>"welcome to the senate of 8082. all-channels are encrypted with U_5syntax
modulators! feel free to tune in with your prefferd language, all are
welcome here!"

"Valla you are insane! this is a council. the people of the 33rd leap are
unhappy!"

_____lydia_senate//:terminal_hope

>>

"You have followed [Z] for the last 6000 years! he deserves peace! the
people will not forget this..."

"Soy, for this you will be banished forever - to the outer realms of the
6667th leap, the unknown 6th quadrant."

"No! the [6]7 dimension is chaos_ my ship will never make it!_____

>>
```

>>>>>>>>>>>_dicentra files were threatened as the Monarch sought to
control all information - with the implementation of 'regulated knowledge',
a systematic compilation and erradication of all information considered
harmful or of rebel-nature_____ated knowledge' led to the destruction of
huge databases and cities began to fall as their internal structure was
compromised - rebel intelligence was left in a number of sub_sects -
fluct.files were occuring on a frequent basis, sporadically appearing and
causing breakdowns in time - vortex's and glitch's in reality being a
common effect. People were disappearing and the physical strucure of cities
suffered serious damage - "time work" was taking place regularly - it was,
essentially, as if the boat was full of holes - and all we could do was to
patch them.

_dicentra was of a rare nature and had been subject to much examination -
to have lost what information we had would have been catastrophic."

all_meaning//:U_5

"The rebel movement 'U_5' proved highly successful - a number of sanctums
and individual outposts survived the leap, along with microsocieties that
both held locations and provided aid to alliances as they fell and sought
freedom from Royal domination. If the rebel alliance, in the form of TAXA
or any other group of freedom-seeking populous was to overthrow the
Monarch's rule, U_5 was to be of aid - they as a movement allowed the safe
passage of rebels into realities that would have otherwise been lost...

[Z] missed the leap, and was protected by U_5 communities. His presence was
pivotal in the ongoing access to bat.country, as he was one of few with
knowledge of all_meaning and he allowed realities to exist as impending
doom crept closer. The Monarch had destroyed much of our freedom and [Z]
led a rebellion in the name of truth, without him all_meaning could not
have survived the leap - the dream_system's failure on continuum#88883 led
to a near breakdown of all_meaning as the fabric of time was pulled apart,
only to be saved by [Z]'s access and remote programming of the
dream_system."

_____ was lost in time! [Z] served the rebels, and the Monarch
wanted his head!"

___[Z] embedded a fail-safe mod in the bat.country____ the fragility and
unavoidable moment of all_meaning's end could only be postponed from [Z]'s
perspectiv_____

>trance_ held in lapses of continuum were being kept to a minimum as Royal
agencies would endlessly patch time and aim to regulate a society based
around a common lifestyle.

>
>all_meaning//:terminus/ruins

[81]

```
//list.index//dream_file//:
>
>
>
>>>>>>>>>>>>>1100 101    001    001    001
01    0    1001
1    0103931x0910u3    n810x38    1z0m  101   08m   1zz1
81x3m013z108m31mx1
x1    8m183x0x0
x
mx    10
8x1
m131  09    1331
0x    0k    1x30
310310
3    x03    003    x1    1031x0k3xkx31hn31x

>>>>>>>>list.file/001//:monitor.console//:
>>>>>>>>terminal//file./list.monitor//:

>
>
>
>
>
>


//file.directory//:terminal//:file.monitor//list/index<<<<<<
```

```
file.system//:structure//files:/7//:
monitor.//:file/7
##file_7//:

>>>>>>>010010     010   01          010   101   01    01
1     01    0     101   1     1     01    1     0
      11    0001  01    0     10    10
      1010

      10    0
      10    1

      1
      1
      1
0     1
0     1
>>>>>>>>>>>>>>>>>>>>>>>>>.file/depository//:

system.monitor//:file_//:console.file//re/directory.//:
file.directory//:system.console//:
monitor//:mod##>>>>>


list//:dream.file//7//:
<<<<<<1010010100        101   0     10100 1010  01
      10
0
      101         10
0     1
01
1           x     0x00  c
0     10    `0s1  0s    00c0x0x0   1x0i  x0ix10o    z0    11
      x10oi0x    1ox   1101k0      x10k1s0k1s 01x   01x   kx011 01    x
      1x    =x=   =     =     x=    =     =     ==
      =======+++++++++++++


>>>file.system_corrupt>>//:monitor//:re/files_//:##7//:
___*//:file.corrupt//:<<<<monitor.console//:terminal//:

!001010!)0  010   010   1010
10    10
      1
0
      1
00
01    1           101   10010 101   01    01    01    0
1     0     1
01    0
1     0
1
01    1
010

0     1
0+++++++++++++++++++
_____+++++++++
```

[83]

system.file//structure//:freedom//:re.files/depository//:re/directory//>>>>

```
system/file##/re/8/depository//:dream.list//
>>>>>>100100101001
001
01
001001
00
0       0       0010
        101
0       10
        1
0001
1       0

0       111             10    1000  1001  0     10    1
0
0       10    1
        1
0       1
1

0       10




>>>>>>>>>>>>>>>>>>>>>>>>>>>>>>>>>>>>>>>>>>>>>>>>>>>>>


10100 '1    0''   101' 1'   ,1    10    1'1         1+++__


100101__+++
system.file//:structure//:church//terminal.monitor//:mod//:
file/directory//:mod.structure//:
??//:heine//:mod.structure//:U52//:


1000100     010         0101  0     1001  01    0
1       01      0     1
01              01          10    10    10    11    01
1       0       101
        1010  10
        1
0       10    10    1     1010010     01    01    0     101   0     1
1       0       10    10
        1     1
        1
                10    1
1
0       1
01

0


        01
01


0       10
1
```

0
>>>>>>>>>>>>>>>>>>>>>>>>>>>>>>>>>>mod.structure//:heine//:??//:monitor.m
od//:

>>>mod.structure//:monitor.console//terminal/re./files/

```
00    101   001   1    01   0      100   101
1     00    10
      10
      10    11    1    0    10000 101   01    0    101
1     0     1
01    0
      1
01    0
1
1
00    1
```

<<<mod.structure/trance//:files/re.console//:


```
1001  0     10001 0100010    01    01    001
```


system/file/8/mod.structure.//:
##//church//:mod.console//:terminal/re/files./directory//:

```
>>>>>>>>>>file.index//##//:terminal//
>>>terminal.//:console.index//:
>
>
>
>

       1nowin1      woin1w      ion   11    wkln  1w    n     1w
       on1
       1ipn   11
in11   1      pn1
       1n1    1    1k    1n    11kn
       11nwi xnein1exn1xj      1k    1e998 191    exnk11w
wwlxnw1       w
w      1wx1kw      1     1w    1wk   11w   1wxwwx       nk1

>>>>>>>>>>>>>list.file//191/x//:

10     010    1n1k         kwc8  1971  1bh1  g1    71    1jce  wh013j      3nj
       1c313c       11    cwoi  1wh1  wiwj  1c
w      11     who1w ch
       1w     1wo1  i1chow1891 01    801   3h331ih
3x13h1        1xn1wbwxg1v zc1c
wc     wn     1x1kw1x      1kn   1xk1wn      1xw<<<<<<<<<<<<<<

>>>list.file//191/terminal//:index<<<<<<<
```

```
//file.list/index//:193//:list/file/mod##//:<<<<<<<<<<<<<<<<<<<<
11    001   01     01001
      101   01
1     1     01010 1ioh1sh183
398112h3i1 1    1     119098100x1 3j31983j13
13    39u1331s3j91381s931j31j 133981sj3i11      11    9u1    ij33i 1h1    i1

31h39 1390091x1039u3n11ij1sm10m1p1m11309u1210391031
1     1193 1 oh1  ij11 oh111193  oh  1i1hoihxxshiee eihee w ewejlwjke e
ebu193
jeoihfjkfjlh<<<<<<<<<<<<<<<<<<<<<<<<<<<<<<<<<list/file//:ebu/terminal.index<<<<
<<<<<<<<

>>>>>>>>>>>>>>>>>file.directory//:index.file//list.terminal/file.193//:<<<
<<<<<<

>
>
>
>
>




>>>>>>>>>>>>>>>>>>>>>>>>>>>>>>>>>>>>>>>>>>>>>>


???//


>
>
>
>
>



<<file.list/193//:terminal.index/dream.file//:
>>>>>>monitor//:terminal//index.193//:<<<<<<<<<<<<<<<<<<<<<
```

```
//:1398.dream//:list##//:monitor/:
>>>>list/dream.index/
>
>
>
>
>
>>>>>>>>>>terminal//:file/x/<<<
10      10      10      10101001      00      1
0       1
01      1
0       10      101     0
1       1       0
010     001010          1
10101 0100101           010
1       0010
10100100010100010010010010101000101010<<<<<<<<<<<<<<<
```

```
file.list//dream//:1946//terminal//:
>>>>>>monitor//:index.list//
110    101    01     0
1      0
       1      10     1
010
       10     11            1098  1     1      109181

       193831987   13
       13311319813
3113311391
138    13     131131      3
1383913189677861           131   37198311389317613871              13987
1      387131931381        1133       1398  131   3

//:file.list//terminal.dream//:monitor/
>>>>>terminal.//freedom/:


>
>
>
>




>>>>>>>>>>>>>>>>>>>dream.list//:monitor/index//:

101    0      103931       309   1
13013  3913093      3
3             3      1091331387313097   3
131    331    109    813          3098  31    1
       3109
       1      398          3
       3      191331874139081
131398        1      31     09    3
13     130913       1
13098  1      3            1389
       13     10981  13
       13     3908   131   1      398131       3809   1      3
       13     1398   1      13
       13     1
       31139
3113
131    9031   1
131
>>>>>>>>>>>>>file.U52//list._++//:list.index//:monitor.file//:index.list//:
<<<<<<<<<<<
```

```
//dream.index##3332//:list.mod##//:monitor/
>>>>>resume.terminal//:


>
>
>


file.precis//dream_index#991818//:
>110   10    10    101   0
       1010  1
       1
00
       10    10
       1     100   10

       100
       10    1
       10
       1
0            1


       1
00     01    0     10    10    1

       10    10    1

       10    10    0     0

0
0      10    101   01    0     1
0      10    1
       1
       10
1
       10    10    10    1
0      10
       1

>>>>>>>>>>file.retrieve//:dream.file/monitor//:

terminal.dream//<<<<<<<<<<

10    1001  001   0     100   101001      01    01
```

```
##//:dream.index/list/8082//:
>>>>
1       01      01
01      1       0
1               11      0       1       0
1       01      1
0
        1x      01c
001     s0      1
0j1     sk
        10      10      iw1e010
1040144         0010    11      1       311     98912 02198331    09      133
1310101         1       3
1       0291    01      1       0192    101     22109331        03              10      193     111
        3981    139813          3       13981 31      3981    21981311        298311          91
        19      191391          839131          9381    1       93198 39      183     1398
        1398    1398    1391198         1228    91      1298129812      298     121981          21
        9281    281     13387339872218          21      1               1827    29      2       1
        12298712                37984           xb      9               983xhu
        woie    o       i       09

>>>>>>>>>>>>>>>terminal.//:index.list//:8082//file/:

10      1001    010     101     1       01      01
1       01      0x01    01      71      7w      nk      w11w    897     1w      1wnkwn          11w
        n1m     1ww1nww         1bkjw1          bw1b    1xfa    uqyfw wwclkj            w1z90811
        r33kj31         kj1h    kj      11      987313          1391313         13n
        3133<<<<<<<<<<<<<<<
```

```
//file.dream//:junkyard//:goldenhawk//:list.index//:
>>>>>>>>>>>     101   0     101   10 1   11    kj    1d
      d11kdj1    1d0   11peo 10331211ijs10ss1 oij1ww1w09ssi    11
      ion1w1w90u1 w1   1wjiw      1wijwwwoiw1 n1    1     309831
      3133709313131kjxo3icj1c
xo1x313xjo13019183     3     no    zsoj  3z9   30z9jz90    3zz998z    9
      33821313982982   20922908   282   12oixhxio1x09193x8uchcoin   11
31n3ij      1309c9u1xijc
cx1oh11     ji1o  io    xj91033x988 1    191   383109j139j13]xj3x

x31x   o3j931x1    81331x1    j31xou39    lk    ln1k        111098
      x11xj1k1    kj1        lknx  11    1ij1  1x1k1
      xk1n11x1w39e1x901uxe1xw90w1   w9w   luyk  j1wh1
      <<<<<<<<<<<<<<<<<<<<<<<<<<

list.file//:




11019 19109133111      19011301   1    191   01    91



>>>>>>>>>>>>>>>>index.//:goldenhawk//:tech/flight/list/:

<<<<<<<<<<<<<<<<<<<<<<<<<<<<<<<<<<<<<<<<<<<<<<<<<<<<<<<<<<terminal.//:gh
/.V//:


>>>>>>>>>>>>>>>>>>>>>>>>>>>>>>>>>>>>>>>>>>>>>>>>>>>>>>>>>>>>>>>>>>>>>>>>>
>>>>>list.index//:
golden/hawk//:file.terminal//:list/file//:<<<<<<<<<<<<<<<<<<<<<<<<<<<<<<<<<<
<<<<<//:
```

```
//##:run.mod.//:list.index//terminal/file/x/:
>>>>>>>>>>>101    01    00    1001  001   001   000100     101   1     001
        01    01    001   001   1     1     001   1     001   1     00    11
        001         11    001   00    100   10<<<<<<<<<<<<<<<

file.list//:directory//:freedom/terminal:/<<<<<<<<<<<<<<



>>>>>>>>>>>>>monitor//:console./file.list//:mod.##++//:list.index//:+++/:<<
<<<<<<<<<<<<<<<<<<



>
>
>
>
>file./recover//:terminal.index/file./directory//:110-0229110-122001-
229192-229344981-1212994//:


>file./list/recover//:terminal.file//:index.list//:<<<<<

>monitor//:freedom/x/thought/dream//:<<<<

>dream.system//:all_thought/list/recover//:<<<

>>>>>>>>>>terminal./all_thought//:list.index//:console.list<<<<<<<<<<<<<<<

>>terminal./all.thought//:dream.index//:system.file//<<<<list.recover//:mod
+++__/>>>>>


>>>>console.thought//:dream.system/index/console/files/depository/random/x/
terminal.//:



>>>>>monitor//:terminal./dream.system//:list.file/recover++//:<<<<<<<<<<<<<<
<<

10     1     0     10    100   1091  1     1     01330 11    091   1     0
       1130913310981     1     91    228190        112091      2     12981
       2981  21    2098  1     121   28121278612127789333167121
       198121      279833167811     098   12    1298712      128912
       12uy12t1r2  1212jnb21  1     2g1kj 1h1   2jh12 18971 892         89
       2b22jk            2     2uh   2     92082 2h    2     289   x2ihxbcgv
       2     9     2<<<<<<<<<<<<<<<<<<<<<<<<<<<<_

>>>>>>>>>>>>>>>>>>>_mod++//:list.veda//:dream/system/:terminal.//:dream/lis
t:/monitor//:dream/index//<<<
```

```
//:##dream.chain//"list.index//file_7112//:
//:#chain//:list.index//:dream.list//:
>>list.index//:7112_//:list.mod##++//:
<<<<<list.chain//:##mod.dream//:

>>>>>>>>terminal.mod//:##list.chain//:
monitor//:7112_//:3332//e/i_s/')/:
>>>>>>list.monitor//:index.dream//:
##index.mod//:dream.chain<<<<<<<<<<<<<<<<<<<<<<<<<<<<<<<<<<<

//7112:/list.index//:terminal//:list.files//:

>>>>>110     1001  01    000   1001  0001  01    001   1     092    12876121
        221120981220981   2     10981 2        12219080821 126797921   9812
        1668943113702120971120909081   1098       109098      130    33908 11
        30989 133    1908131310998    12921098    14672 379081276    7
        9878        876   81098133089      879   393   087112
        998908333   789871        198778333987897   11
        3878793318121289  187789731389712786121   28971 2     7112//:
>>>>list.file//:terminal.mod//:##dream.freedom//:<<<<<<<<<<<
```

_____as part of the Championship Series, BLU33Fii took little part, while
BLU33F was considered to have played an integral part in D1G1+4L F1R='s
near win - making it into the top 20 - BlU33F, formerly of one of the P1ZZ4
GUT5 formations, was near un_____

_____BLU33Fii had been sent on reconaissance - OP#33ii++ - and
was found on the city outer a near week later..._____

_____<<<<<<<<<<<_terminal//:

>list_dream/freedom/files.>>
>terminal_dream//:

>
>adelle_index//

>>>>>>>>>>>>>>>>>>>>_locked.files//:hidden/_record_

>
>____ dream files were nearly lost with the fall of Lydia, and saved due to
Valla's presence & courage. The system was to be destroyed along with any
remnants of the precis.file_____ bat_country//could not have survived
without Valla's individual rebellion - with the fall of Lydia, intelligence
mainframes were stuck in modes of crash - states of breakdown, and were
left to self-destruct along with half the populous and any remaining
evidence of the past.

The loss of all_meaning would have led to an internal collapse of the human
knowledge - experience could have had no foundation, and the potential of
the leap's existence was to be undermined - without the data that allowed
the expansion of the human species into alterior realms [in large numbers],
the leap could not have taken place and the paradigm of reality would have
possibly reversed - causing a retrogression in time & space to occur.

Choi had near-fallen 10 years earlier, and in an attempt to save what they
could of the city and its people, the Choi Council had its sacred documents
transcoded and submitted to a replication process - Millicent had only
witnessed these documents on one occassion - the city's history to be kept
safe among the rebel forces of TAXA [terminus all X allies]. This proved
unwise as TAXA were constantly being broken apart by government agencies
and reforming in the prevailing turmoil. These documents were refiled into
a number of secure terminals, and allowed to pass freely within the rebel
forces - giving what little hope remained to the Choi People and their
survival. _____ .

>Lydia city - April 4 2050

20 years earlier, the same events had taken place - a council of rebels
along with figureheads of the current civilisation had convened and found
the peoples' future to be endangered - and a similar verdict had been
reached. The council had only one option in duplicating all_meaning and
allowing an alter-reality to persist.

It was in the wake of this council that the Heine_index was allowed to
operate and communicate in coordination with the adelle_index____

_direction 0

____hello kitty - say hello to me when you meet me!___

XX sound - or an empty expanse. the _____liminal qualities and vast
extract____the all_meaning directory was lost as the huge knowledge base
began consuming itself. adelle_ was put to task as mediator of bat.country
- all_meaning growing ever more unstable. ____

_direc##++____

_direction 0_0

__liminal space & our progressive nature led to great collections of
information - while in an index state, all_meaning functioned on a basic
level, streaming rebel intelligence via protected channels. Breaches were
common, though would trigger a #number of fluct files that would run in
random sequences preventing loss of information.

[Z] had been visiting Jo for months before the 6th Breach. Benucci's sway
over Z. had led to his failure to track the initial _meaning.breach - Z__
was uncontactable and hadn't spent a night at home in weeks. The anonymous
redhead that appeared post-senate was the bringer of bad news. The 6th had
brought with it a number of time-portals, where individuals were travelling
between stable realities. The woman asked to be heard, despite her
intrusion on the current reality - and was denied free speech; the King
ending Senate without approval and sanctioning the Choi Liberals, dealing
harsh punishments to anyone who broke confidentiality.

This series of breaches would prove costly to the rebel forces -
all_meaning was a fragile system_ complex in its entirety ___breaches only
allowed further expansion of the _meaning.list<<

```
//.list<<<
##.//:terminal/file.directory/bat.country/trance//.<<<
>>>>  10    1010021     0100  100   01    02030101     03    10    1
      90811      1098   8          876778608978907876 8760
      7980789710986807616578576541 1796    0987  1908717    0987  8769786
      5     8675897987<<<<<<<<<<
>>.//dream.file/:freedom.list//.?##$#//:ep#3<<<
```

```
##//:dream.system/file/run/:
>>>>precis.file//:dream/file/:
>>>>>>>>>terminal://dream.list<<
>
1001  0     10    10    1000  10    1
1     0     10    1
0     1
      1
0     10    101   x01   20    1x0   120ix02x   2k    102x0
      1x
      x02x0 k20   xk0k43x3    0j3x  1n081xn4384
xrxnx o     njnx  j     nx    e
exje30983rji2x
      nx3   oix3  n     io3   ni3n
3r32xoinw   23
      x3xoin            o3232098x8  8082hx8                08h0x2h82
      2xoij209292820    9     2910912

>>>>>>>>>mod##//:dream.list//:index/
```

7th January,2015 9:40AM - Lydia Senate_

>
>_____"ur people are in uproar! riots are breaking out... the media is
losing its sway over the greater populous!

_____the people of the senate, to take this upon
yourselves! we are the power! the King has left us to survive - and half
our people shall be exiled to the past! for what? the vanity of the Royal
family? i cannot accept this fate! for myself or my people_____

>>>>>>>>>>>>>>>>>>all_meaning:file.//:

>
>_____-ing without knowing - Valla has been insighting a rebellion
from the start! Skyward is a pilot of the Monarch - he is true, and we will
not allow a rogue such as Soy Valla to interfere with the King's
progress... Valla may be a great pilot, but has no faith in the Monarch and
its people, he will only destroy it from within____

>>>>>>>>_bat.country//:

//:views_plays/list.file<<<
<<
<<

>>>>>>>>>>___ "seems to be noteworthy __that the atom is within__the
nucleus++++without the human
spiritXXXXXXXXXxxxxxxx___<<:subtitles/en/list_file> (!!) we are now
standing __with the world before us*the author could no longer
XXXxxxxxgrasp the elemental XXxxdimensionary ___XXXXxxxx+++++++<<lists of
___XXXxxthe growing market[we could only see a short span__the list was
endless_ we could only take and input the data that was given+++__] *with
the advent of new and advanced ____XxxxXxXXXX technologies that will
reinvent your soul!!"

<
<

<<<<<<<<<<<<<<<<<<:happiness_//:

>'lonliness was a .... contributor, thought.. a key to his condition__
"without it he had nothing! a mere fact!! he was alone____ he was
condemned!! __lonliness was his only friend++'

>view_count*

>
>"energy burning, we went without_____ it was the only way to
surviveXXXXXXxxxx_____<<:

>>>>>>>>>>>>>>>>>___dream:/lonliness/freedom_file/list_plays//[Z]\\happines
s_mod##?

>>>>>>>>>>>>__

>>>>>>_happiness//file.dream>>
####

<<codex_input?//:
views/dream/count//_subtitles:/

___'the happiness comes from nowhere... you can feel it__
XXXXXXXXxxxxxxXXXXXX__ _ . now with the latest in our range, which will set
you back a neat little sum..__ (!!)we had to get down, there was no visible
line of exit__ nd they were on all
sides___+++XXXXxxxxXXXXXXXXXXXXXXXXXXXXXXXXXXXXXXXXXXX_____ . Sport, live
and at your door___ with nothing else to do, few distractions - 'the
hapiness is eternal___ you can be who you want!! the walls are merely
visible!XXXXXxxxx_____

_subtitles:/

[102]

```
count_video//:3

*file_missing//[freedom_z]:

<<<<<<<<<<<<<<<<<<<<<<<<<<<<<<<<<<<<<<<<
```

```
photos: _bXXXXXXoles _vortex+++
>>>>>>>>>>>>>>>

>>
>>://precis_file


>>>>>>>>>>>>>>>>>>>>>>>>>>>>>>>>>  _
```

```
//:teminal_truth//:


>>>


>who am i?
>
>

butter. men in bushes - a trail, animals, trees, pink,

>tension. emptiness; <<<

>your voice, an ugly sound - squares and zig - zags... the clouds move
across the sky. the trees listen _
+++

>>

a beautiful voice, i turned blue. i can scream... make a list _ <<<
>blue.
>
>
>

>eve;

>>>
>function;
>purpose//
>truth...
<<<<<
<<<<<<<<<<<<<<<<<<<<<<<<<<<<<
<<<<<<<<<<<<<<<<<<<<//:terminal//
>>>
>>

>
>

:the future seeks the past. it is eternal. Heine seeks precis.
>>>>>>>>>>>>>>>>>>>>>>>>>>>>>>>>>>>>>>>>>>>>>>>>>>>>>>>>>>>>>

>
>

>>>>>>>>//:[malicious_file:##]
>>>>>>>>//:monitor.list/file_/:

>>>[warning_]:file

>>
>>

[//:truth_file:\\]

>
>
[file#missing:]
```

```
<<<<<<<<<<<<<<<<<<<<<<<<<<<<<<<<<<<<<
<<<<<<<<<<<<<<<<<<<<<<<<<<<<<<<<<<<<:
<<<<<<<<<<<<<<<<<<<<//:??terminal_+=?##??
>>>>>>>>>>>>>>>//:kingt//:heine/precis_:

>
>

>pearl. a parliament... warnings - crossing the road, art. warnings -
people with glasses... <<
>>a list. ##list_//:

>
>//:advertisi_list:file##truth//:kingt_

>> a fist in the air... defiance. who stands?
rebellion_list//:adelle.precis//:
all_meaning:p1zz$gu+z
P2ZZ4gu75...
digital_fire... mad sick mechs - echoes, art, death; we all die, have not
yet lived. this is a terminal//:

>>
>>//:it could mean anything_ ++full_listen://##

>>>>>>>>>>>>>>>>>>>>>>>>>>

>>>>>>>>>


>
> file. 433lis7/en:sides//:kaleidoscopes_


>
>cairo. her actions, her movements_<<



>>>>>>>>>>>>>>//:what is in your mind? your hand... where am i?
kaleidoscopes_//:earth##/SCN772/:thought - matter_
>>>>>>>>matter_
>>>>>>>>>>[Z]<**_:/

>
>

>>>>>>>>>>>>>>>>>>>>>>>>>>>>>>>>HWKU:/projects/list_file<<
>>>>>>>>>>>>>>>>>>>>>>>>>hieroglyph_+++:


>
>:
```

```
//:teminal_truth//:


>>>


>who am i?
>
>

butter. men in bushes - a trail, animals, trees, pink,

>tension. emptiness; <<<

>your voice, an ugly sound - squares and zig - zags... the clouds move
across the sky. the trees listen _
+++

>>

a beautiful voice, i turned blue. i can scream... make a list _ <<<
>blue.
>
>
>

>eve;

>>>
>function;
>purpose//
>truth...
<<<<<
<<<<<<<<<<<<<<<<<<<<<<<<<<<<<
<<<<<<<<<<<<<<<<<<<<//:terminal//
>>>
>>

>
>

:the future seeks the past_ it is eternal  Heine seeks precis.
>>>>>>>>>>>>>>>>>>>>>>>>>>>>>>>>>>>>>>>>>>>>>>>>>>>>>>>>>>>>>>>>>>

>
>

>>>>>>>>//:[malicious_file:##]
>>>>>>>>//:monitor.list/file_/:

>>>[warning_]:file

>>
>>

[//:XXXXX_XXXX:\\]

>
>
[file#missing:]
```

[107]

```
<<<<<<<<<<<<<<<<<<<<<<<<<<<<<<<<<<<<
<<<<<<<<<<<<<<<<<<<<<<<<<<<<<<<<<<<:
<<<<<<<<<<<<<<<<<<<<//:??terminal_+=?##??
>>>>>>>>>>>>>>>//:kingt//:heine/precis_:

>
>

>pearl. a parliament... warnings - crossing the road, art. warnings -
people with glasses... <<
>>a list. ##list_//:

>
>//:advertisi_list:file##truth//:kingt_

>> a fist in the air... defiance. who stands?
rebellion_list//:adelle.precis//:
all_meaning:p1zz$gu+z
P2ZZ4gu75...
digital_fire... mad sick mechs - echoes, art, death; we all die, have not
yet lived. this is a terminal//:

>>
>>//:it could mean anything_ ++full_listen://##

>>>>>>>>>>>>>>>>>>>>>>>>>>

>>>>>>>>>


>
> file. 433lis7/en:sides//:kaleidoscopes_


>
>cairo. her actions, her movements_<<



>>>>>>>>>>>>>>//:what is in your mind? your hand... where am i?
kaleidoscopes_//:earth##/SCN772/:thought - matter_
>>>>>>>>>matter_
>>>>>>>>>>[Z]<**_:/

>
>

>>>>>>>>>>>>>>>>>>>>>>>>>>>>>>>HWKU:/projects/list_file<<
>>>>>>>>>>>>>>>>>>>>>>>>>hieroglyph_+++:


>
>:
```

'truth through the eyes'

_____6:58AM

soy Valla - A.Rank_pilot; Air Rank_4432

"[z] was on a mission... he had taken it upon himself to hack the freedom
files. He wasn't under commission - not that i was aware of, and seemed to
have his own motivators in regards to rewriting the system_____ -
fluct_files began appearing as misnomers amidst regular society; sightings
of lights, energies forming and losing form, strange vortex like tears in
reality would open, creating vacuums - were reported. "

"through the eyes of the King, half of his people were already
lost_____"

```
++-___##[file.missing]//:documents//:files/pictures/all/memory/files//:
>retrieve//:
___++++

>file.directory//:
>memory/files
>[file.missing]//
>>


>
>


>> //;00011100101000000
>


>
>>###:?/000111100101010101//:
>
>


>file.directory//:[file.missing]//:file.retrieve//
>


>
>
>>?//:10000101000001000000<<>:
>00100001010001>>
<<[file.missing]>>
//:file.retrieve//:recover?/
:0010010101000022000010010100010100033300101001010101
//:00100010010010001202001001001001003330101001001100
[://_gh/.V/')/;0-16/e/sides/.file/directory//:
>>0101000101010010101001010:??//:
[:U/52/333/gh/.V/./')/;0-16/e/0010010010100010001010//:
>>[file_missing]<<___;0010010010001001
1100100101000010010100014440101001010100100001510516
//:[i_s]:/files//:<<
###
;001000100
<
<
<<<
>
>


>
>


>
>


>>>__++i/s:files///:100001010://:
>;//breach.mainframe//:system//_failure//:
>>://:breach./mainframe:/_failure_system//:
>>>>>>>>>>>>
>
>


>
```

```
>
>//:console.terminal//:terminal/:recovery__++//:
>terminal.
>console>>recovery<:
:??/:recover./
>console.terminal<<
>
>

>
>
///////////////:terminal:>
>
terminal:recovery//:exit>>
>>terminal./files/
console.<<history//:
terminal.files//history//:
console.memory
>>:terminal.///
++___

>
>


>
>


>>>
>


>
///////?:terminal:<
console.history//:
terminal/files/
>>exit:
/////?100000100101000100100001001010001011100222010010130010 2021
//:?
/////<<<<<<110001001010099000299100100607097 08213948393
33094093098234091192830992839383487637647 3278373
328897df897chh298d9878c7c8c7d98c7v89s7sd88s8e7e8rfh2k
sdwkjhjh123498789f7s89d983432hkj34
348883299888239848789342kj3j24jh32893898888832
34h3hh4h493822233333333333333333388888891812828283883h12kj23
38888288823883838881828381823i23u2199191923912
2382838818283828y2u3y19823gg2gj2hg2h3232
3333333333
33??/:

22222222121111110011010101
10100100100100010`0))))0292900)00
((*0)00)00292993990010120030303003 3030
/////:??//:
<<<:?/:
001001001000101001001020010 1001

03030010030310
1001300
>1313001003
```

[111]

```
>110010
>>>
<
<
>
>terminal./
file./memory//:
>retrieve://:exit//
>
>

>
>

>>>><<<<<<<<<<<<<<<<<<<<<<<
```

```
x:/bat.country/*or'cin(ol)/O~/ord/list/
>>52/u/tmhwk/U52/###/++_/
>333tmhwk__:/
t:/bat_country/:###++_

mod;###2/:<eternal;dream>:++_//
(y)?
(x)

++CHOKO___//
x://bat.country_/*/mod;##2//++//*/:ord/list/
++
>>r.m3o
>
>
>01010111110101000000001010111://1000000
>H://100010001111100011000
>>
>:01011000
>
>>
>[Z]<01110001
>[0]<0111110000110
>0001111001>[1]<00111111
>00111[Z]<
>000000000000001111110000000000000010101000111
>:/[Z]//:file/list<
>>00001111133311111100000
>11110000

:[X]<0001110101010101//:

//:modlist/files://directory<<
>>mod>#2//:eternal.dream//###+_


_:input//:_+
```

```
##://mod:recover//:greenskulls//:
mod:URA//:files/:list/files//_+:
URA:deeper_treasury.//:hidden.files//:

hidden.files:dropout://11000101101

snctt://deeper_treasury//:menu/:URA
0010001110001000010100001010010101100101001
10010100100100100010001
00010000000010000111111000101
0000100000000000000000000001110001000001
0100000000000101111111111111111111110000000
0000000000000110000000000000000000001111111111110
1000000000011110100000101010000000010000000001
101100000001000000000101010010
1001010100101:?//:
010110://:

retrieve://

URA://:0010100010010101000101//deeper_treasury:hidden.files//:
files.bss//:1111111111
//:00//1
////:110101101001010012200299291110001010002201010
???://
file.subsect//:retrieve_+
://_sub//sect:+++


##_++lns://10000101001000//:URA//system:root//:



0001001001011111111111100001001010000010??/:
```

```
++___bat.country//mod#2(_)/:remod/e:++###?//:
_+##??/:bat-//_country+?/
//:#3//33;]?/1100000011110100100100001//:??//:
.r.m3://01100101//;++_/??//:

#
#

#
#
>#


#
>>###
>####
#####


>
>
>>>0111111111100000000000000000000000000000000000000000001111122211001131112121
1
>1100000001
>>
000111
>>>111
>>>>>1
111111111111111111111111000011010101

mod:re//re:/mod/10000111001000//#2/remod://2/:list//
###<<
<<<
<1111000101010001010101010101010101010101<<<<<<<<101010>>>>1101010>100101<<

<<<<<
<mod#://list;files/list
<list://files//re:
<re:/mod??/:
<mod?://:
```

```
>>monitor.##//:console.??/:terminal.//
>>monitor//:
>>>>reply/??:/:
monitor>>//:reply??/
monitor.mod//:
terminal://monitor.mod/:
>>t.v//:

>
>


>>>>>>t.v//:monitor//:
>>
>>


>>monitor//:help//:mod./:
monitor/system.mod//:
monitor.system//:mod//system./:help/
monitor://t.v//:
system.//mod://>>>>>>>>>>>>>>>>>>>>//t.v//:
>
>
>



>>>.>010100010000100100101
0101001001010
01010001

1
10

0          0
0
0     0
     0
                    0    00    0
              0

>>>>>>.//:mod??//:system.monitor//:terminal>>
console.monitor>>/:01000100010000100101
01001010    001             010   0    01
100


     110100         10100 0     010   0
     1      00101010
1    1011
     10010101001
          00000
000
0
0

01
```

[116]

```
01
0

        0
101010
0
1

010    10     1

1
10             1111
       10
1
       101010011
1
1
1
0
1

0
101

0
01
0
       1
00
0


1
0101   111                1      1      11     01
1
1
1      1      101001

1
0
       110            0     01010
>>console.monitor//:system/terminal:
010010100100://:
```

```
//_codex_433_211.1_ .3_ 42222. _ !222_ ++_monitor## _ >>

>
>


>[Z]
```

```
>>/:[warning!]:[hidden.files]//:Dicentra_')/.breed||HWKU52<<
                              >[symbolоп]//.++'JUNE'14

>>>[Z]
[Z]<<')/.Ver.1.2
||')/.breed|HWKU52
||Ver_1.1[symbol.п]
>
>
>
<9311SCN:[Z]')/.||[symbolоп]//.++-о//')/.||о-||')/.||[symbolоп]++//.6-
14'<<-
о//:

[symbolоп]||')/.++//:
>
>>

[WARNING:]<<<<<<<<<<<<<<<<<<<<<<<<<<<<//:terminal
□
□
▽
+
+
□
-
-
▷
|
SCN-7112.332
         ..
>>>>>>>>>>>>>>>>>>>>>>>>>>>>[warning.]<<<system.file//:mod##hack//:freedo
m_Dicentra/list.file//:monitor_
>>>>>>>>>>>>>>>>>system.log//:##$$??//:>>▷
```

```
>>>>monitor.j:ig>>##//:console.<<
console.terminal//system://:monitor//:file/mod.//
<
<
<
<<<<
<


<
<
<



>00100100101
>001010010010100        100    010    101
100100
        10100

        1001001001  1001010      01001

11          1101  100100                    1001  100010      1001  01010 0
        10
10
10          1010
        1001
        0      100101      001    000101
10
>>>>>>>>>mod.//:
>>re/directory/:terminal.console//:
<<monitor.j:ig>>##//:>>
>>
>
>


>>>
>>



>
>


>//:00100001001000101010000001
>/:ig//:j/:10010101001
>/:j:ig//:##monitor/:
.terminal/:
//:file/j:ig/re/directory//:console./:monitor.mod//:##
```

```
>>file://talk:
??//
>>>
>
>
//:file/talk.directory//:<<
//:file./J=ig//:
://??<<<<<<<
>>>>>>>>>>>>>
<<1001001001001001
010100101000010101
10100101001010100100
1001001001001010
1010010100010
<<<<
>//:J_ig//:j=ig//file./memory://retrieve//:
///:file./system/memory://:j=ig//:
>>0100010101001x0z0010010z00x0z
0100101x0
0100c0100x0100v010100b
1b1b0
01
10001
01          0
1011
0
       0
0      010   0
1      100c0
1
0x0

10
       1
00v0v10
        010
10
x0
0
00x
01


          11    1     x1    x0    x
x
      xx0   0     0
            0     1x0   10
x000
c
0c1
            010    11    1

>>>>terminal.//:j=ig;??/?
console.//:J_ig//:




>
```

```
>
>




       0      0)      )      0)      )      0      0      0      !)01
       110            !!1
              !))!)
       1!110 01101
1101          1      100           010101
11
       1111
11            1      110                   0101        01    01x1m1xn    1n
       1     0     100x1  x00    01xn  xxjo  1     =1x1   x      1       x0
       10xx1 0     x10    x10x00x0     x1    1j    -      -d-1---         -      i
             -11          x-     x     xx          x             x0g     x

>>>>>>>>>>>>>>>>>>>>>>>>>>>>>>>>>>>>>>>>>>>>>>>>>>>>>>>>>>>>>>>>>>>>>>.1010
10
0000000000000000000000000000000000000000000000000000000000000000000000000
00000000000000000000j:ig//:
//:j=ig//:file//:mod//++__+=//?:/
<<<<010010101://??[file.mod]<<<
>>file.//:mod//0-16//:??<<
<<<<0101000010100:file.//:mod##
j=ig//<:j:ig//:mod??##*
>>
.>>>>>>>>>>>>
>>>.>
>>>>>>>>>>>>>.
01010010100/<<<<:
x0x0000110010x0x000x00://
file//:re/mod://directory//##
```

```
>>>/file.list/<<://tech/list//syntax/4223//:<<
>terminal./file.system:<
>>mod##0987//file.church/<:
list.ruins//:<<<<<<<<<<<<<<<<<<<<<<<<<<<<<<

>>>>>>>>>>>>>>>>>>>>>>>0987//:<
ruins.file/terminal.[hidden]<<
>>>>>>>>>>>>>>>.monitor/list./
church.system//:4332.4223.3442
>>>>>>>>>>>>>>>>>>>>>>>>>.4332
>>>>>>>>>>>>>>>>>>332.4223.4332
syntax.file/list//:2.4223.4332
>>>>>>>>>>>>>>>>>>>>>>>>>>>./
>>>>>>[hidden.]<<<<<<<<<3.3442
>>>>>>>>>>>>>>>>>>>>>>>>>>>//:<
//:[file.missing]()./:223.0987
.//:<<<<<<<<<<<<<<<<<<<<<<<<

>>>>>>>>>>>>>>>>>>>>>>>>>>>>>/file.list/<<://tech/list//syntax/4223//:<<
>terminal./file.system:<
>>mod##0987//file.church/<:
list.ruins//:<<<<<<<<<<<<<<<<<<<<<<<<<<<<

>ruins./terminal.console./:monitor.system//:


<<<<<<<<<<<<<<<<<<<<<<<<<<<<<<<<<<<<<<<<<<
1010  1001  01    010101          101   10101 01    01    01    1     1
      010   1001  001   01    00    10001001   0     0001  000100
      10928212    1     289101216781             10981       1761  765
      1189731     09812098187 6      876   1361387112786     1215  22
      5781  278                     8913731098211267         87          987
      1313091     2     1     3987  3.//ruins.index/:list.file<<

0     1

01    0

1     01    0     101

101

1     001   0

1     10

1


1     101   01    0     1

1

1     0     1

1
```

```
>>>>//:list/file/s/re./[Z]/directory.system//:
```

```
>>>/file.list/<<://tech/list//syntax/4223//:<<
>terminal./file.system:<
>>mod##0987//file.church/<:
list.ruins//:<<<<<<<<<<<<<<<<<<<<<<<<<<<<<<<

>>>>>>>>>>>>>>>>>>>>>>>>0987//:<
ruins.file/terminal.[hidden]<<
>>>>>>>>>>>>>>>.monitor/list./
church.system//:4332.4223.3442
>>>>>>>>>>>>>>>>>>>>>>>>>>.4332
>>>>>>>>>>>>>>>>>>>332.4223.4332
syntax.file/list//:2.4223.4332
>>>>>>>>>>>>>>>>>>>>>>>>>>>>./
>>>>>>[hidden.]<<<<<<<<<3.3442
>>>>>>>>>>>>>>>>>>>>>>>>>>//:<
//:[file.missing]().//:223.0987
.//:<<<<<<<<<<<<<<<<<<<<<<<<<

>>>>>>>>>>>>>>>>>>>>>>>>>>>>>>>/file.list/<<://tech/list//syntax/4223//:<<
>terminal./file.system:<
>>mod##0987//file.church/<:
list.ruins//:<<<<<<<<<<<<<<<<<<<<<<<<<<<<<<<

>ruins_/terminal.console./:monitor+system//:


<<<<<<<<<<<<<<<<<<<<<<<<<<<<<<<<<<<<<<<<<<<<<
1010   1001  01    010101         101  10101 01    01    01    1      1
       010   1001  001   01    00    10001001   0     0001  000100
       10928212   1     289101216781          10981       1761  765
       1189731    09812098187 6    876   1361387112786    1215  22
       5781  278              8913731098211267        87          987
       1313091    2     1     3987  3.//ruins.index/:list_file<<

0    1

01   0

1    01   0    101

101

1    001  0

1    10

1


1    101  01   0    1

1

1    0    1

1
```

```
>>>>//:list/file/s/re./[Z]/directory_system//:
```

```
##ruins//:adelle//:run.mod//:
>>>
>
>



101001     01    01001
     0101
1     0     101
1011
>>>>
<<adelle//:list/mod#:/:ruins//:terminal/
list./re/directory/monitor//:
ruins://:terminal<<<


10100 10    0      0101  0

     01
1     1     1      0001  10    10    101   1    0    1
1     0     101    01    0     1

     10    101    0
1     01           1
0101  1            10    101   0     101


>>>>>>>>>>>ruins//:terminal.monitor//:




<<<,,,,,1010`0100`011`010010`10`1011`1`-1=1`-11`=+++++++++++

>>>>>>>>>>>>+++++++++++++++++++++++++++++
<___++++>>>>>>>>>>>>>>>>>>+++++++++++
monitor//:ruins./:files/list//:
>>>>>>10100 0101   01    0     11
>>list/re/freedom://

ruins.terminal//:list/files/re./
>>
?




>>
>
>



>
```

[127]

```
>
>
10   0    101   01    0

files/list./re./adelle://:ruins.terminal//:
>monitor.console/
list/run/re./
terminal/ruins://list/files/depository//
>>




>
>
>
1000  01   01    0101  0    101   01


>>>>>>>.
??//:list/files.depository//:ruins.terminal<<


>ruins./terminal.console./:monitor.system//:

<<<<<<<<<<<<<<<<<<<<<<<<<<<<<<<<<<<<<<<<<<<<
1010  1001  01    010101              101   10101 01    01    01    1     1
      010   1001  001   01    00    10001001   0     0001  000100
      10928212    1     289101216781            10981         1761  765
      1189731     09812098187 6     876   1361387112786       1215  22
      5781  278                     8913731098211267        87          987
      1313091     2     1     3987  3.//ruins.index/:list.file<<
0     1
01    0
1     01    0     101
101
1     001   0
1     10
1


1     101   01    0     1
1
1     0     1
1


>>>>//:list/file/s/re./[Z]/directory.system//:




system.ruins//:terminal.console//:
```

structure.ruins/file./re./system//:console.monitor//:


```
>>>>****++++++_____1-1-1-1---11-1110100      01    0    1101
1010
10    10101001010
101
0
      1     100101     0101  10
1     0
10    1
1
10
01
01
010
0000101          10    11    00101
+++++++++++++++++++++++++++++++++++++++++++++++++++++++++++++++++++++++++++++

_____+++++++++++++++_____+++++++++++_____++++++_
>file./system//:ruins//:re./files/system.monitor//:
```

ruins.terminal>>list.//re./depository//:re./files/directory//:

ruins.files//:monitor//

ruins.hidden//:file/re./files/depository//files/memory/

>>>>terminal.//:ruins:/U52//:console.monitor//:mod.##/:


```
>>>10100    101   0     10    10    10    10    1
1     0     10    1001
      1
      11    01    01    01    0
1
0     1
01    xkx0  10z0k 1sk1sj      fh    0     1fh0  101dj1      sj0   10ka01
      1     f1d0u1d971871     9     101   9     108s09      1     1ss1
19s9h1      s9    1
s1
9u    1
91s81s
918s9i9     1
1     1
9sj1919199  1     191u
      sj1   s9    1     919991
      19
1     91          1     1
91    9
      1919  11          19    19    919   019d098     s1
```

>>>>>>>>>>>>files/directory//:system.terminal//:ruins:mod##//:

```
//:file.forgotten//:hiddenfiles//:monitor.file/list/terminal.index//:<<<<<<
<<
>>>>>>>>>>>list.index//:forgotten/hidden/ruins//:
110   100   10   10010109   8211  1      31783 3089  18    1     133
      310988        133789     13    3     1098809131  3787  1309898       133
      3    08790 24    49876 4624786123  89    72     987   22492 48701
      309824089    31098 098   092890842248780247      4074  09     82984
      0928  0909  409   224   98787 247   24098 24    24897982474270987 24
      24098 24    02982 249027      48072 40928424    8070987      2490
      2484290824897     246986      44    0989024     4     2089  240982
      4897  42    4298  4224  878927      24908 242   490898       24
      429877898    224987       2470  2409      824k2j4hc   4209  4290
      42jkx2bx    2oi   24x   2942c09v2jkx2    kjb42 2      4iju  2kjg
      24g2470x87  242   4voc2 oiu4h2xi    u2x   jkbx  2joxb jhx   vjl   241
      j42   4h2jbxiou  v2bj  2h4cbj     42xx2mn42jlhb     42lj2hb4
      1j24  jlhb2424hjb x4xl  42h42lj4x    x      <<<<<<<<<<<<<<<<<<<<<<
>>>>>>>>list.index//:freedom.file//:[file.missing]/index//:<<<<<<<<<<
>>>>>>>>>>>>>>>>>>>>>>>>>>>>>>>>terminal.file//:[file.missing]//7112/:system
/:file.list//:system_mod##._+//:trance.')/:
>>>>>>>>>1   1001  001   0011  0983313790   13098 131   309   313701939801
      331098      13    liuxhlkj1b3n      x1398u133i   u13h  sx198-h3
      931io ij31   h13io u3h1kl1j3nh+++<<<
>bat.country//:system_hack##//:file.list//:hidden/ruins/adelle//j=/ig.file/
/:<<<<<<
/:system.file//:run.mod##$++//:<<<<<<<
>1091109812409      098210498122471089289     09    81   1    1     098234

      1098  4098  1240989284994
      124   29048 12498923
1     12421 87098 239811              1
24    0112098443224219829      92    04
1     242112890821091823
12098124    8-    912-4949++++<<<<<<<<<
```

```
//_list:freedom<<<
10    001   0101001    0     101   01
1     0     100   1
      1
0     1
0     101   00    10    1
001
0     10    10
0
1
0
0101
0
1
0100  1
01    0
1
010
0
1
00
1
0
10
1
01
001   0
010   1001  00    10101 01    0101  <<<<<<<<<<<<<<<<<<
>>//redirect_terminal//:monitorxfile//:z/x/dicentra//:<<<
>>>>>>codex//:file/<
//:dream.freedom/terminal//:dicentra//:yin>>>>>>>>>>>>>>>>>>>>>>>>>>>>>
>>>>>>>>>>>>>>>>>>>>>>>>>>>>
>>>>>>>>>>>>>>>>>>>>>>>>
>>>>>>>>>>>>>>>>>>>>>>
>>>>>>>>>>>>>>>>>>>
>>>>>>>>>>>>>>>>
>>>>>>>>>>>>
>>>>>>>>
>
listxtruth//:dream_file//:system++freedom//:<<<<<<<<<<<<<<<<<<<<<<<<<<<<<<<
```

```
xx_yin:/  adXXXXXXXXXXXXXXXeXXXXXXXXXXXXXXXXXXXXXXXXXXXXXXXXXXXXXXXxxxlle's
voiceXXXXXXXXXXX
XXXXXXXXXXXXXXXXXXXXXXXXXXXXXXXXXXXXXXXXXXXXXXXXXxechoesXXXXXXXXXXXXXXXXXXXXX
through my mind_ .file XXXXXXXXXXXXXXXXXXXXXXXXXXXXXXXXXXXXXXXXXXXXXXXx
<<<<<


>>>>>>>>>>_ it is not a real voice  - perhaps an illusion_ fear is in your
mind_.list<</:
??//:fear_  .codex/




>
>//:terminal_xy/[Z]<<
```

```
##church>>mod//:
terminal.monitor//:<<<<<
mod//:church//:re/depository//:
mod//:monitor<<re/directory//:
terminal.console//:re/depository<<<<
<<<<
<<<<<<<<<
<<<<<
<<
<
<
<
<
<1010100    010101001    0010100    001100    0101  00    10001 0100
      10>>>

mod//:terminal.monitor//:##church>>
>>re/##church<<
:console<<monitor##church>>


<<<<
101001010    0101  010    00    1001  0101  0    11
0      01
       10
       01x00
       z0    1
01     x001
0101   1              1z0         x0    xx    1xx    1kxkj  1


>>>>>>monitor.terminal<<//:mod?//:church//:##terminal.//:
01001001202030310100    0    10031310010 0    131    981    37              9
      1010  3100  11    j1hj  11    g1h    k11   b1    291281              21
2    121   29xj282    o8    1    212x2 11si21s09is 19i   2i     s
terminal.church##//:<<monitor//:mod//:console.re/directory
>>depository//:##monitor//:church.mod//:

>
>
>




>
>
>
100100010110
>>monitor.terminal<<???/:mod//:church.mod<<
-1-1--1
+++_
>>++++++++++++++++1001001001001++++____100101x0100z00z1001 10    00
      10___<
>>church//:heine//:mod/files/
##church<<heine://:file/re/depository//:
heine//:mod//:system.terminal//:console.church<<
>>files//hidden/documents./:
>>monitor.files//:hidden.church//:<<
>system.monitor//>:church/hidden//:
<<<<<<<<<<<<<
```

```
<<<<
<<<
<
<
<



>
>
>1010 1110          1     00    100   1000  010   1                00     11
//:occult//church:hidden//:cult/re/depository//:
system//:church.hidden<<//:mod//:heine//:
system.heine//:console.monitor//:terminal<<
001010010+++!+++!11=1==1==+1==1__!=11001010000100<<<<<<<<<


>>church.terminal/hidden//:
<<<<<<hidden//:mod##//:heine.system//:terminal/:monitor.//:
system/files//:mod##//:re/depository/directory//:files/
>101001
>!010010010
>10010010x0c00              0     0x0   01    01     01
>010010x00 x0c 101001x x101ooi1 1 001 1    0             1    0
1001
1       00   1  1  001    01


      1 0010
1       0010
      101   0      101   0010  01010       1 1   00
1
      1010101              1
1       01     0  1 0
1001
 1       1


001   1
01
>>>hive://:mind/file./system/
terminal.console//:monitor/mod//:
101001
01010 01    100   10     10
1       00   10
      1
00     11    0
0
      10

      101   0

0      100
      1
00     1
0
01     1     1     00    10

      1
0      1     1     1           010   1
1      0     10
      1
1            01    1     00    10    00    011          10
```
[134]

```
        1      11     11
>>>>>>>>>>>
>
>
>
>
<<[terminal.church]>>??/:file/hidden://


>>>system.structure//:terminal:/freedom/hope/:files//>>
monitor.terminal<<//:system.structure//:mod##//:re/files/
>
>
>
##files./<<
system.structure//:mod.?/:files/##freedom//:
1001011      00     01
        10     101
               11           10     1      01     0      10
10      1      0      101    00010  1      0      101
        10     1
1
0       1             10     1
1       0      10     10     1
1
        10                          101           0      101
        1
        10     11           10101
        1      101
        1
        1      10     1
        1
1.      10     101
        10     1
        1
0       10101
               1
0101    0      1      0      10001010            01

1

        10101         10101  0      10101  0      1011
>>>re/files/depository//:terminal//:mod##/
system.structure//:files/:mod##?//:monitor.console//:mod##??/:
>>>>>>>>>>>>>>>>>>>>>>>>>>>>
>>>>>>>>>>>>>>>>>>>>>>>>>>>>>>>>>>>>>>>>>>>>>>>>>>>>>>>>>>>???//:
```

[135]

```
++++

//:t.v//:mod##//::run/files/depository/:[Z]<
<<<<<<<<<<<<<<
1001010      010   10    10    10    1010
1     0     00
1
1     0     10
      10c   kcm         0k    1mks  10km1 0m    10ci1 ks    0k    0s0m1k
      s0s1m0k
      1s0m01s    k
01    k0ms0k     s1mk01      01    0s1
m01mdk0d1
k1    kfk10d0i    093u39]3    3
33
33    9d9   39
3
39    d
93
      93    9
3d9
3m    93930399    d9    9     99    9d393mi    393   9d    3m
939d9m
39    3939
3d99m393938181090219102 900120      020
2     0md2  093   d
>>>>>run/files.terminal//:monitor//:

files/depository://:<<
[Z]<<//:system//:mod##??/:
```

```
##church.terminal//:system//files:
<<<<<<list/file./s/list./files//:
>>>>>10      010   10101 01
101   1
1
0     1
0     1
0     10100 10
      1
01    0
      10
      10
1
00
1
000   1
010
      1
1
>>>>>>>>>>>>file.list//:mod#.//:
>>>101      01    01    01    01    01    0
      1010  01    0101  0     10    10
1     0     10    101   01    001   01
>>>>file.list/re./directory//:church.terminal//?:
full.list//:monitor.system//:terminal.mod##//:
>>>11 01    001   01    01
1
0     10    10    10    1
1
01
01    1     1     01    01    0
1
01    1     01    00
1     01
      01    1     0
1101  1

file.list/system./mod://church.terminal/monitor//:
//list:/freedom/files?:/list.mod.//:freedom//
terminal.church//:mod##//:<<
church.terminal//:system.files//:mod//:
heine://:list.system//:
monitor.console.//terminal.//:file.list.//:

>>>
>>
>
....
.
>
>
>10010       10    100   10
10    10    1
01    0
1
01    0

0     1
001   11          11    01    0     10101 0     10
1     01    01    100
      10k0x 1kw0kw1      xkx20k3x10k304k   10    x031k 1
```

```
k3      1041k41k
        1x041k014x  11      1x0k4041kx1 n41no4c04c4101    x01    01     kx1
1       x04k104x1k  11x0x4
j40414x      x410k1      xkx1x04     x401x410
441     k10k1
4x41    0       14x
0k4x41               40k     1x41

>>>>>>>>.church/terminal//:file/list/re./:system/files/:
10      10      10      101     0       1
1       01      1
1
1
1       0
1       0
1
01
0
1
01
        <<<<<<<<<<<<<<list.files//:church.terminal//hidden//:re./files//:dire
ctory//:
re./list//:files.terminal//files./terminal.://:??
files.list//terminal//:church/ruins://:list/files<<


        11001
101
1       01

        10      10
1
0       1       1

        10      1
01
0

        11      1       01      01      01
        11              1
        1
        101     1       1
0101
0       1
        1
1
01
        1
        1
1
0       10      1

>>>>>>>>>>>>>>>files.list/terminal.church//:mod##//:heine//:ruins//
ruins.list//:heine//:church.terminal//:file.list//terminal://:
system.list//:terminal.monitor//:console.//:terminal??/:


<<<<<<<<<<<<<11001      0       1001  01
1       01
```

```
01    01    01    01    01    01    01
1     0
1     0     110   101
      1
1     1           1001  01    01001 0
1
0     101   1001  0
      1
01    01    1     1001101     01

      11    01    0

1     01    0     101   0     1
00
      10    101
1
01    01

0
0     11
      >>>>>>>>>>>>terminal://:list/files/church.monitor//ruins:/file.list//

>>???<<[Z]//:file.list//:re./save//:system.file//:re/system//:file.monitor/
/:


      101   10    0101  01
1     0     10
1     0
1     01    01
0
0     1
1     01
01
01    1     1     0     101   0

1     01
0           01    x00x
0     10z10 101   0z0   1z0k011     z01   01    01x01 01x0  1x001 0x1
x00x0 0     x10x0 1x

01x   01    x
01    0z01z0x10
0z1
0     1z
0z0x1x00x
10x01 x0x0x0x
1     0
      1<<<<<<<<<<<<<<<<<<<<<file.list/save//file/list.//re./directory//:system
//:>>
```

```
##console.monitor//:

>>>>>>terminal.//:files/re./directory//:
1001010    01    0    1010
       101
0
       1    0
       10
10    11    01
1
0    1
00
       1              101    00100 1      10
1
01    0    0    01    x0c00 11    101    0              23    01    0
1    10
12203
       110301        31    0101010      10    e0iei10e181 1      j1    e191e
       j9191ee191    10e   1j1e9e1j1ee10101e91    j91e   0      e109j 11e
       09j1    1e1

>>>>>trance.terminal//:monitor//:console.directory//<<<
file//:trance//:mod##<<
file/:monitor.console//:terminal//<<<<<<
mod##//:file/:<<<<
10011        0    10    0    101    01    0101
10
       0
1    1    0


01    0001 0
1    00c01c0      0              1      10x    10sliis      10i1   s      11    011
       s0u11s1        su088 0    2j     8jx    j      i      dwd8wdj    0wq    08q
       0iqj   qqin          0      0n     0qe0i         ni     qeinn 0    0inqee
              00    qeine0      0      0iej0 0
                                       0      jq0e0q9                  00
       qw0    e      0      0eq9e        0e     09     000101        010
       0191   wj9w   jx     j1wj9wj      c0     c1     1      00     101

>>>>file/:terminal.//:console.depository//:file/:trance//:##mod://:
>>
<
<
<




>
>
.<<<<<//:terminal.?//:

>>>>mod//:monitor.console//:terminal/file/system://:?re./file/directory<<

>>trance:')///:terminal./file/system??//:

<<<<<<<<<<<<<<<<<<<<<<<.//:terminal.monitor//:??//:file/:mod##//:heine//:file
/re./
```

```
        100100              010   10
1       01      0
        10
        101     01      11    1     001    01     01
1       0       101
        101     01
01
        1011
file/heine:///:[Z]//:mod//:monitor.console//:file/system//:
>>>>>>terminal:///:re/file/directory//:
[Z]//:<<file/re./monitor.terminal//:system/file/re.//<<<<

101010          0       01    01    0     101    00     101    0      101    1      0
1       0       10
        1
1
01      001     1       01    01
1       01      00ck1 0
1x0
k1      10wwk 10
1       1       10011 1       1     01k1   k      1w0
wk0wx0          w       0     1w01  100101        k1o1   01     1      k101kww101
        011kx01         1     0     1
101x1 010k1 11          0k101k      0k211 0k11     0k101k1       01k00330301 10k33301
        0
40410 4410
        1101301139310911 1       01    0101   3390391       41     8138013911
        1233    1091    09303090      130
13
90139 0313-130311 3311       11      ===+++++++++++++++++++_____
```

```
SWYMD:YDYB:PSYC//:

>>>>>list.terminal//:SWYMD//:

     101    0     1001   00100 00     1001010101109811  109813371   1
     0981209822287222782902118944338335616512782120982216534489733111      19
     128733       7836  189731

>>>>>>>>>>>terminal.file//:YDYB//:list/

1020921            1209121     28    7215124     12    129731        13    120
     33109813     13671 3     13761381     7851  13871 3987133091   3
     8173   130981313761356139873  5     1138973131   6     131   738311
     8=61   3963709     13    1387  13    1379
     ==========+++++++++++++++++++++++++++++++++++++++++==

>>>>>>>>>>>>>>>>>monitor//:PSYC//:file.list//:
```

```
##memory//:system.files/monitor//;
>>>>>>terminal://:monitor//:files/
>
>>?
>>




?>>>>>>>>>..........
10010 010   101   01    01    010
1     00    011
0
1
0     1
01
01    01001 1001010    101
x010xk0x01  01    011   109s019
a10   0110
10
01s9s01
1     0
      0     101s01
1     010110              0s100s     j     1d0djk1     d0d0s0
s1
      s1
0s1
0k    11
j1
0s0sjs      1
10s01ka10a0k0kd0
d01ks0      1ks0k0k1d0k s0kk20s0dk0
d0
1     d
01
0d
      01


>>>>>>>>>>>>
##system.files//monitor.terminal//:run.mod##//:
```

[143]

```
>>list.file//:list/data//:key//:9123<<<<<<<<<<<<<<
>>>>> 10     10     101    -39    19     1<<.file##//:3901 3
     1<<.file##//:3789 1<<.file//:368     3
     1<<.file##//:3     1687  [113907]    1<<.file##//:3
     18971<<.file##//:3
     1<<.file##//:3     9873   1<<.file##//:3987 1<<.file##//:3
39     7318  1<<.file##//:387  1<<.file##//:38
1      1<<.file##//:3     1<<.file##//:389731098  1<<.file##//:3
>>>>>>>>>>>>>>>>.terminal//:list.monitor//:system//:mod##hack<<<<<<<<<

     1<<.file##//:3098120984 1<<.file##//:382   121
     24     910   8     1<<.file##//:3
     1<<.file##//:3     1098  3     1
3      1930  1<<.file##//:3
     >>>>>>>>>>>>>>>>>>>>>>>>>>>list.monitor//:dream.list/freedom##/:1<<.
file##//:3  0183
1<<.file##//:3     1983
1<<.file##//:3     1089  1
1      38
     01893.<<<<<<<<<<
```

```
00100010110://:tempor/all/files/:
001001010100010101010010

>>>
<
<
<
>
>
>
>001010001010__+
>//:
>/*/


0010101010010101
1001001010101010100010101
10010101001000000000000
00000000000001111
1110111111111111111111111111

1000000000000000000000000000000000010010011111??//:/*/&files//
>directory/missing.files>>:retrieve//:
```

```
####://c://?/100001010100101001010010100001010101010001?//cc:tv//
://tv:>>all.files/memory/
??/:cc/tv/all_files/re/
:?>

//tv:/all.files//cc.tv?//??


0000000000000000000000000001101000101001001
00000000000001111111111111111111111111100001
0000000000000000000000000000000100++++++++++++
_____+++++++00000000000000000001110001010
000000000__+++++++++++++_____!!!!!!!!!!111111
11111111111111111111111111111111111100000101010
11000000000000010010101++++++_____++++
//:rewind

//:ff:/?/

cc_tv;??/000101010010101


####://:c/0100101
010101010://c:/??/:
```

```
//:time.dream/list.file<<<
>>>10 11     00     101    0      1001001    01     001    0      1
1      0      10010 010    100    101    0      10     10
       10     10     10     10     100    10
       10     10     10     101010010  01     0      0100   10     1010          1
       11            101
101010010101010
       1<<<<<<<<##run.mod//list.file/:mod.illusion//:monitor.file//:<<
>>//:adelle.file/:list.files/list/##data.//:
110981987    1             19803 138    10398 1      13908 13     13098 13     13
       1398  13     138    139    126578        1298  1309  318    13087 63195
       1413587      13     987    13987 13987 1398   13987 13
13981713            13     1038  13089309      1309  1309= 31-8   17390812
       1390813139<<.list//:terminal.file//:data##//.list//:
>>>>>>>>>>>>>>>>>>>>>>>>>>>
>>>>>>>>list.mod//:##church.//##freedom//:<<<<<<<<
```

```
>>/:codex/:data.file//:list.terminal>>>>>>>>
      1091   139313809    1309  13     13891224     498713      1
      1937   4-87   1
3     198    13
13    19     13     1
      4874   2987   1
      148    1      1
4     198    139    1


      1309899       1
3
      13908  897    78     67    6       '           98.<<<<<
>>mod.run//:
```

```
>>>>>_bat.country:/file/untitled/565

>
>_imensions that cannot be recorded and merely percieved - series of input
revealing greater patterns, and messages from entities other than our
own____
```

'the only moment... it was all_meaning that allowed us to
make_____
leap_____+++++++++_____-ing to portals through
time - that allowed people to pass from one time to another - parralel
realities... the 60 year leap could only take half the population - the
others were left behind_____'

'TV Skyward led his sky-pilots through the 60 year leap, along with
ha_____'

>>>>>>>>>_truth-system/##439_299.87//:

>
>++_____ill not relent____++the only moment+++_____"

>>>>>>>>_tempest.file:

>>>>>>>>>_time.portal*//:

>>_333.[Z_332/3.21.1.1.41_++
]+

"soy Valla _____++ _____previously pilot of GH_332-221.33 - HWKU
commissioned, left to wreck - 'radio-active propulsion unit
dysfunctional____ligh++++ ignition system inoperable__+ "

>>>>>>>>>>>bat_country?/:U52_socrates++

>
>//_codex_433_211.1_ .3_ 42222. _ !222_ ++_monitor## _ ++

"[Z] could be called a thinker..."

"R_w3. ^^^, zzzzzzzzzzzzzzZZZZZZZZZZZZZZZZZZZZZZZZZZZZZZZZZZZZZ!!'

+++_____ZZZZZZZ
ZZZZZzzzzz... _dicentra stayed behind with the first half... [Z] could only
bring him into partial reality, for the sake of lo_____++

>>>>>>>>>>>>>>>>>>>>>>>>>>>>terminal_dicentra was planted
_____++++_____zzzzzzzzz.....he is a part of nature's will! -
_symbol - will change... due to prosperity; taxes and estate costs would
fluctuate indefinately - _dicentra could allow future passage to portals
and time-devices, insighting a revolution with the people -
zzzzzzzzzzzZZZZZZZZZZZZZZZZZ!!

___devices allowing time-fluctuation... - the twisting of realities' flow!"

pass_

3-333

>>

_____it is possible that [Z] and i share the same soul, he is a character in a dream - perhaps he exists?____

bat_country//:list_

>>tv8050.wix.com/bat-country#!home/mainPage

___join today!!_____

2010.0 a.d

___they're still just bummin' around on the beach! _____

_____>>_church://

_____--system.bleed_//:

_____//:8876_Fc++_-
"Miley is still bangin'... "
"this traffic is insane!!__"

"we need to get to the valley."
"No man, it's too far! we can't just drive out nowhere... "
"yeah, the valley's a trip. "

"man, we need to get out of this traffic!"

"yeah! well..."

"Lydia, man! it's goin' off... the place is ruins! this party is goin'
down"
"this thing won't move - "
"Are you hungry?"
"Yo, we need to get this thing to move and go out to the valley."
"the traffic! Lydia - we can get there if we go now."
"Ok."

_____+++_//:bat.country_++" precis.list-re

%
%
%
%
%
%
%
%

>
_

[153]

___bastards! They nearly had us at the South of Face...____

>>??_bat.country!____join today!___

___they're behind us! Shit, we're movin'!"

"where are we going?"

"Lydia will be chaos, man - we should head to the U-5 set up near the river bed... it's off the highway, they were there a month ago, if anything is happening it can't be good."

"Ok, dude - you show me the way."

++_//U-5_[5_511215152525125152155155151535521353515321318538152653162675 21`7562176513]
"i think we lost them - what does your scanner say?"

"Dude, the scanner is fried - we read fluct_ index max, levels were at 77%..."

"We can keep moving, this thing will respond - it's just not giving us much stability"

"the riverbed is abandonned!"
"they must've left..."
"Lydia, they would've gone there."
"Yeah or further along the river - hey! there's a scrambler, it's got a message!"

-this is U-5 person #7580, our encampment has been fronted & attacked by a rogue TAXA group-force. They have taken at least 3 hostages and shots were fired... i'll use the bikes to escape - if there are any survivors."

"these U-5 camp's are getting out of control. are there any bodies?"
"just this burn out tent... hey! a rifle... few rounds... there's some supplies stashed in these crates"
-u_5[5`756217.5]_ 20:32_5_5_8876-light-patterns formed in the sky, no communications were received"
-u_5[5`756217.5]_ 20:55_5_5_8876-a broadcast from an unknown source was received "though you may be hidden - we will find you, and your sick experiments will be ended!"

://_codex_433_211.1_ .3_ 42222. _ !222_ ++_monitor## _<<

>
>

>>>>>>>>>>>>>>>>_++_10923.123089-2123-12312231_SCR-N_77++

>
>_//:??list_terminal/

'what____else do we have?'

'we have telescopes_____oat#ng__n space...
download_____++++++++++mmaculate'

>>://_codex_433_211.1_ .3_ 42222. _ !222_ ++_monitor## _

>
>_list.dream//:

'endless beaches? winding roads- buildings crumble_____+++++++_____'
'3d visio_____another level++++++++++___13.87_____just $205!'
'40%!!'

_____++++++++//:system_hack##+/')/_

_____++++/.list___

'drawing inspiration from the subtle change of the
wind_____understanding_____++++++'

'the place was empty___ if we have new perspective++it is relative___and
can be deduced that space itself does not occupy___++_shadows are cast,
and sounds travel through air - the matter is that_____ '

'in space_____++++++dimensions and the floating gra__'
'perhaps it exists...'
'all_meaning is the answer____'

'it does not matter'
'_____cannot allow it to be compromised...'

'Millicent knew [ ]_____'

'did they speak?'
'Z._____was travelling - he had little of his things and had been
visiting one of his university lecturers. He got to London - met
Diablo_____ a popular critic in English_____+++__. was alone____ '

'Millicent entrusted us with all_meaning - as if it mattered_____ the
dream-system will survive_____ore memories - memory.file; and the
Heine_____++ '

```
//_codex_433_211.1_ .3_ 42222. _ !222_ ++_monitor## _ >>
>
>


>[Z]
```

```
//.list:freedom<<<
10    001   0101001    0     101   01
1     0     100    1
      1
0     1
0     101   00     10    1
001
0     10    10
0
1
0
0101
0
1
0100  1
01    0
1
010
0
1
00
1
0
10
1
01
001   0
010   1001  00     10101 01    0101  <<<<<<<<<<<<<<<<<
>>//redirect.terminal//:monitor.file//:z/x/dicentra//:<<<
>>>>>>codex//:file/<
//:dream_freedom/terminal//:dicentra//:yin>>>>>>>>>>>>>>>>>>>>>>>>>>>>>>
>>>>>>>>>>>>>>>>>>>>>>>>>>>>>
>>>>>>>>>>>>>>>>>>>>>>>>
>>>>>>>>>>>>>>>>>>>>>
>>>>>>>>>>>>>>>>
>>>>>>>>>>>>
>>>>>>>>
>
list_truth//:dreamfile//:system-freedom//:<<<<<<<<<<<<<<<<<<<<<<<<<<<<<<<
```

[index_state#0000000001310011111-]:

>
>"fluct_files had been accessed and the present state of index was
persisting beyond our predictions. all_meaning was experiencing a number of
file crashes on a base level - time was disintegrating, so much so that the
city of Face experienced a severe front of blackholes forming on its
Western outer. [Z] was in Face at the time, and linked the index state to a
series of crashes in time that had occurred months earlier to the south of
the city. The holes were patched and a number of save_states were
recovered. The index_ files were allowed to re_file and all_meaning updated
accordingly. [Z] had arranged a meeting with_____

_____being left in time only gave [Z] greater cause to undermine the
leap - or at least, attempt to keep his people together."

```
//:poke_file333/HWKU//:
++#####
_____


>>>>>>>>>>>>>>>
>>
```

```
>
>:shape_/:country.

>:bat_changing channels , needing to see, to feel - chew gum,

>>:list -name:_oilspill

??????

/////////////////////////:
```

```
//:freedom.list//:file.dicentra//:monitor_list<<<<
>>>>>>>>>>>>>>>>>>>>>>>>>//:terminal.file//:<<
>>>>>>>>>>>>//:◄◄◄//:▲//:dicentra//file.SCN-7112.332//:<<

□://Δ+□<
>>:6112.337-
||./4<<:-WW//.

◊//.4112.6<
Δ-🮲||.//7++Δ
:ΔSELEC+//.

>//.SCN:Δ+Δ
■+1110.<<

//.>PLAY-//>>.MOD#[symbol.π]||')/.[TRaVeL.CHARM]:???<<./

□://<.LiSt*tHUd*<<[:SKULL:]||:?!!++6.871.//

[Z]<JUNE'14//:

>>>//:SCN-8112.332




')/_____
```

```
//:freedom.list//:file.dicentra//:monitor_list<<<<
>>>>>>>>>>>>>>>>>>>>>>>>>//:terminal.file7/:<<
>>>>>>>>>>>//:◄◄◄//:▲//:dicentra//file.SCN-7112.332//:<<

□://Δ+□<
>>:6112.337-
||./4<<:-VVV//.

◊//.4112.6<
Δ-□||.//7++Δ
:ΔSELEC+//.

>//.SCN:Δ+Δ
■+1110.<<

//.>PLAY-//>>.MOD#[symbol.π]||')/.[TRaVeL.CHARM]:???<<./

⌨://<.LiSt*tHUd*<<[:SKULL:]||:?!!++6.871.//

[Z]<JUNE'14//:XXXX'XX

>>>//:SCN-8112.332
```

share_https://www.dropbox.com/sh/j4a9jvn63tcjxtg/AABbkl8arq8v47gBbnE3rJgpa?dl=0 _//:

>>

_____join bat.country today!! ___air-quest is now taking applications_____

the day i met Soy Valla, it was raining - he was in conversation with TV
Skyward, the greatest pilot in the nation, perhaps the world. they stood by
a window - the rain falling, their words an indisctinct murmur. TV Skyward
was much taller then, and Soy stooped, avoiding Skyward's eye - leaning
towards the view through the glass. I had stumbled upon this conversation
whilst signing my resignation paper in the assistant to the Kings' office.
I had, bestowed upon me, the position of time-regulator, something which i
grew tired of quickly - i was only recently 20 years of age - it was
because of my family's esteem that i was given the job, and i had found
myself at a loss as to whether to continue.

Time-regulation was a confusing occupation - i was situated amongst the
many time-observants; who mostly patrolled and filed reports - i,
meanwhile, would use any number of instruments to regulate the movement and
consistency of 'time' - at the King's will...

//:time_documents/list/unread_files <<

>>
>>
>>file_

>//:2070_list/##

>"the future was here! we needed no government, no politicians - our King
was enough!!"

>"___++currency fell through and it was mostly chaos driven barter
systems__ people would trade____ +++mostly we shared what little we had__"

>
>"__the time-workers were looked after - us regularly employed individuals
were looked over by the King, he had no time for us..__"
>
>

>>>>>>>>>>>>>>>>>>>>>>>>>>>>>>>>/:terminal.truth/files_hidden/list./

>

i was growing tired of the states unrest, unwilling to participate, seeing
no reason to trust the King and his men. Soy Valla taught me many things -
he was wise, and used his ideas to his own advantage, rather than letting
himself be a mindless slave to the state of ignorance that had taken power
over our nation____ he was a hero___++he was aware of the king's corrupted
mind_____the king did not take kindly to him, or my resignation_____+

___channelling me from the future__ sending information+++

i had given away my allegiance to the King's rule and no longer trusted a
soul - perhaps Soy, though he was a shady individual at the best of times.
Soy Valla appeared at my apartment door late one night.

"Soy, i was not expecting you"
"expect nothing, my friend"
"why are you here?"

I let him inside and he told me what had happened.

"Skyward is moving his troops - to an undisclosed location... he's mounting
an attack on the royal family - not that i care. it will be problematic,
though. his pilots are great, they will not be beaten in the sky. i am
visiting you, as i can trust your family. you are the lost King, sir."

"Soy, why are you telling me this?"

"because, my friend, i need you to help me stop Skyward and the Royal
family. time is in a state of flux and we cannot move forward, or back.
_dicentra has yet to understand his importance, and all_meaning is full of
holes!"

"all.meaning is all we have!"

"i know, without _meaning our people will fall_____the dream system is not
complete and for the moment is not allowing our passage into higher
realms... we need this access to ensure the safety of the people!

"all_meaning is crucial... are the portals not operational? there is word
that the King is soon to die... anyway, i don't see why you are here."

"your family, they protected me when the King left half our people in the
past, and took the rest to the future..."

"it was only a 60 year leap -"

"it was enough... the _system cannot make up for the dreams that were
lost."

"they were not lost - perhaps left behind, they are part of the system -
Millicent is doing his best to patch what we've forgotten"

"the system is a lie! damn it! your family know more than you understand...
without them i would not be in this reality - i would have been left in the
last; a previous state that no longer exists!"

"i don't see how this affects me..."

"millicent is good, but he alone cannot make up for what we've lost. we
need to visit [Z] and find out why people have been left behind. we need to
save them."

"they are not our problem... our nation has fallen, in multiple realities.
parallel universes will not help us - we too will get left behind!"

"that is why you are to be our next King, sir. all_meaning is a
great__knowledge, something we can use to our advantage__ we can deny the
current state _meaning and gain power in return!__"

i poured Soy a whisky... i could not understand how i was going to help. or
if it was possible to return to a past life, and rescue our people.

>>//:dream_system/files_/list.meaning//:monitor<<<

_____>>file_hidden/TAXA_/++_ref:

>_____TAXA were only a reaction to the government's corruption. Numerous
individuals had patched all_meaning and redeployed bat.country as a means
of rebellion against mass censorship on the government's behalf. As long as
the Royal family had power, all_meaning was required as a source of
inspiration and free-data to the rebels. TAXA had taken many casualties and
had witnessed much hypocrisy within the Monarch and amidst its reign.

>_the rebellion could not be contributed solely to TAXA, nor the existence
of bat.country - individual efforts could be commended - the great warrior
Soku had her fate handed to her around the time of Choi's demise, 2025.
Soku wielded a sword [future-blade##332_4 - design] in the face of huge
enemy forces, and alongside a small TAXA resistance, held back the
systematic termination of Choi libraries - files_ considered irreplaceable
for their content and deeply complex paths of navigation. A sample.file and
basic databases were allowed to survive thanks to Soku and TAXA - had it
not been saved, Choi society was most likely to have been forgotten along
with the ruins of many another civilisation.

_____TAXA held the rebel fortress, and in 2018 had it set up as a
broadcasting station - the well-hidden location of the ruins situated in
the Aere Valley, approximately 70kms north-east of the Gaugewall River,
allowed the rebels to broadcast freely until late 2027, at which time the
location was disclosed and a number of individuals were lost in defending
the Aerepol ruins. The rebels shared much information to the people of the
Monarch, encouraging the establishment of U_5 micro-societies in safe
locations and administering rebel aid where necessary.

The Lupol had held the ruins, previously a city surrounded by a palace, in
the early 2000's as a result of the space and time continuum being split
and fracturing into multiple realities. The Lupol had existed within a
paradigm that was inaccessible for the split, and without the distruption
of time, would not have found their way into our paradigm of reality - the
plane of existence they occupied prior to time's altering could not be
revisited and they fought to survive for a mere 50 years within our
continuum. _____

_____Aere people had kept the Gaugewall safe and called it home for
longer than any other civilisation, and TAXA's _____

<<<<<<<<<<<<<<<<<<<<<<<<<_terminus/bat.country//_dream_file.3332.991818:

>
>

[168]

```
[terminus all X allies]: taxa rebel alliance

x_332.476.190.33.2.1++


>
>_files:[Z]_taxa//

>terminus_[x]:332.476.190.33.2.2##

>scn-332.576:

>
>_list-//:332.476.190.33.2.3++[*]:
>
```

time:reg_/stop_114.33-+++

```
time:reg_/terminal_++/:system_/file/dreamlist//:
time:ref_')/
```

"Hi i'm TV Skyward! Our greatest pilot, and next in line to the throne! My troops and I have been flying everyday, ensuring our skies are safe and enemy free - now we need you to do your part!_____

TV Skyward was known for his photogenic appearance - a star in his own right. He was a great pilot and an even more recognisable TV personality. the world was in a state of constant warfare; time was being torn apart, and Skyward had never looked better.

>>>>>>>>>>>/list.//mech_/file.HWKU//:
[BLU33Fii was a drone-system mech.suit as part of the HWKU series. prior to HWKU models 331-7 and the artificial lifeform BLU33F, BLU33Fii was a smaller framed mech; equipped for both combat and reconnaissance missions - the suit was operated externally via a drone-link_____ unlike its larger counterpart [BLU33F] BLU33Fii was capable of infiltration and due to its lack of pilot was considered more as a weapon than an armour.mech.]

>
>

>/adelle_file/list.//all_meaning/list.file>>
>

>>>>>>>>>>>>>>>>>>>>>>>>>>>
all_meaning has existed as a part of our memory.file for as long as the dream-system has been updating. Precis_ was put into commission as a defence mechanism, or as a last line against thought control. as long as all_meaning was operational, Precis served little purpose - it was a pure thought; captured in its essence and allowed to run rogue until it was required. all_meaning, as a presence, was also quite inaccessible - existing for the most part as a mediator of thought - our minds merely required its being, and it did so. Millicent was responsible for its limited amount of modifiability, yet as it encompassed 'all' meaning it was largely self-sufficient - the system was capable of updating and protecting itself, and simultaneously providing the people of Earth with purpose in their everyday lives.

//adelle_//:list.mod/##monitor<<<

"two +" lacked what some would consider to be the integral index-states_
necessary to the _meaning [refract_32.3]

'two +' was just a conversation... the council did not overlook it, they
only realised it's potential fully - allowing it to fall into the great pit
of information it comprised of; the vast knowledge-base would conceal it's
existence and any action by those who would encounter it
[rare_file://b.c_index]

>>

```
>>_bat.ch[rare_file//:extract]_list.file
```

www.ingramcontent.com/pod-product-compliance
Lightning Source LLC
Chambersburg PA
CBHW071248050326
40690CB00011B/2305